THE UNOFFICIAL HEROES OF OLYMPUS COMPANION

The Unofficial Heroes of Olympus Companion

Gods, Monsters, Myths and What's in Store for Jason, Piper and Leo

Natalie Buczynsky, Jonathan Shelnutt & Richard Marcus

Ulysses Press

Published in the United States by
ULYSSES PRESS
P.O. Box 3440
Berkeley, CA 94703
www.ulyssespress.com

ISBN: 978-1-56975-986-8
Library of Congress Control Number 2011926034

Acquisitions Editor: Keith Riegert
Managing Editor: Claire Chun
Editor: Richard Harris
Copyeditor: Bill Cassel
Proofreader: Lauren Harrison
Interior and back cover design: what!design @ whatweb.com
Front cover design: Double R Design
Back cover design: what!design @ whatweb.com
Cover images: blue background © yobro/bigstockphoto.com; Zeus
    coin © Tektite/bigstockphoto.com; gold background © t_kimura/
    istockphoto.com; ship coin © Jaap2/istockphoto.com
Interior images: see page 191

Printed in the United States by Bang Printing

10 9 8 7 6 5 4 3 2

Distributed by Publishers Group West

IMPORTANT NOTE TO READERS: This book is an independent and un-
authorized fan publication. No endorsement or sponsorship by or affiliation
with Rick Riordan, his publishers, or other copyright and trademark holders
is claimed or suggested. All references in this book to copyrighted or trade-
marked characters and other elements of books by Rick Riordan are for the
purpose of commentary, criticism, analysis, and literary discussion only. The
works of Rick Riordan referenced in this book are publications of Disney
Hyperion Books, and readers are encouraged to buy and read these books.

To J.C., who makes me believe
that I can do all things.
—N. B.

To the one who makes
Zeus look like a tiny spark.
—J. S.

To Eriana Marcus,
still the brightest light illuminating my path.
—R. M.

Contents

A note on spellings and pronunciation in this book: Ancient Greek was written in a different alphabet than we use today, and through the ages and various translations, a number of different spellings have been used for their names. We've elected to follow the most common spellings used today, and those used by Rick Riordan in his books. The versions we reference are:

Riordan, Rick. *The Lightning Thief*. New York: Disney / Hyperion, 2005.

Riordan, Rick. *The Sea of Monsters*. New York: Disney / Hyperion, 2006.

Riordan, Rick. *The Titan's Curse.* New York: Disney / Hyperion, 2007.

Riordan, Rick. *The Battle of the Labyrinth*. New York: Disney / Hyperion, 2008.

Riordan, Rick. *The Last Olympian*. New York: Disney / Hyperion, 2009.

Riordan, Rick. *The Lost Hero*. New York: Disney / Hyperion, 2010.

CHAPTER ONE

THE GODS THEN AND NOW

GRECO-ROMAN GODS and goddesses can do a lot of miraculous things. They can make themselves tiny or huge, transform themselves into any animal imaginable from serpents to swans, hurl lightning bolts, appear and vanish at will, or turn the tides of battles. But there's one thing they cannot do: They can't die. They are immortal.

THE PERCY JACKSON STORY

This simple fact is the central premise for the Percy Jackson & the Olympians and Heroes of Olympus series of young adult novels by Rick Riordan, a former middle-school

English and history teacher from San Antonio, Texas. If the gods of antiquity could not die, Riordan reasoned, then they must still be around . . . somewhere. Probably not atop the original Mount Olympus in Greece, where they would stick out like sore thumbs among the thousands of tourists who climb that mountain each year. Nor would they likely reside in Rome, which is now the home of the Catholic Church and long ago rejected the "pagan" gods of ancient times. No, the old gods would most likely live in the heart of Western civilization today—and that, at least to an author born and raised in Texas, could only be the United States of America.

With that in mind, in 1994 Riordan wrote *The Lightning Thief*, a tale designed to introduce adolescent students to Greek mythology in an exciting new way. The book features a troubled 12-year-old hero who suffers from learning disabilities—dyslexia and attention deficit hyperactivity disorder—and has trouble keeping out of trouble in school or even staying in the same school for more than one year. Upon discovering that some of his teachers are not what they seem, Percy is forced to flee to upstate New York, where he takes refuge at a kids' summer camp called Camp Half-Blood. This is no ordinary camp. It is run by Greek gods in the guise of mortals, and each of the kids there is a demigod—the offspring of a mortal parent and a god. Percy soon learns that the very flaws that caused him to be seen as a troublemaking nerd in the outside world are the traits of a hero in the realm of gods and demigods. Soon he is off on the first of a series of quests with his friends—Annabeth, a daughter of the goddess Athena, and Grover, a young satyr, or goat-boy—which will take them across the breadth of the United States and bring them face-to-face with gods and monsters that have lived since ancient times.

After several years, Riordan succeeded in finding a publisher who would buy the rights to *The Lightning Thief*, but the book was not actually published then. Instead, the rights were traded from one publisher to another until finally one editor noticed that Percy Jackson's story bore a striking resemblance to that of Harry Potter, the hero of the British novels that rank as the best-selling young adult series of all time. That was around the same time author J. K. Rowling announced that the Harry Potter series would come to an end with the publication of the seventh volume in 2006. Booksellers, educators, and fans alike began to wonder nervously who "the next Harry Potter" would be—and behold, the long-unpublished *The Lightning Thief* surfaced.

In the years since, Riordan has written a new book in his series each year, just as J. K. Rowling used to. Although his books have yet to reach anything like the universal popularity of Harry Potter, each of them has reached the top of the *New York Times* Best Seller List. And just as J. K. Rowling is credited with introducing a new generation to the joys of reading, Rick Riordan has undoubtedly succeeded in his goal of bringing the adventure and excitement of ancient mythology to millions of young readers who otherwise would likely roll their eyes in exaggerated boredom when the subject came up.

Over the course of the five novels of the Percy Jackson & the Olympians series, Percy and his friends matured from age 12 to 16. By the fifth book they were getting a little old for the kind of summer camp they'd known so far, and in any case, Camp Half-Blood was no longer what it had been before the final apocalyptic battle between the Olympian gods and their ancient Titan rivals. So Riordan immediately set to work on the first installment of a new series, the Heroes of Olympus. This book, *The Lost Hero*, introduced a whole new set of young characters. It promised to explore the transformation of Greek mythology into the mythology of the Roman Empire. And it assured fans around the world that, as the series progressed, Percy Jackson would be back.

HOMER AND THE HEROES

The Percy Jackson phenomenon is the latest chapter in the timeless saga of the Greco-Roman gods and goddesses, demigods, and monsters. The origins of the gods are lost in the mists of time, long before the first of the ancient Greeks were born, but date back to earlier civilizations such as the Persians (4000 B.C.), Northern Indians (3100 B.C.), Mesopotamians (3000 B.C.), and Egyptians (2600 B.C.). At least one mythological being common to Egyptian, Greek, and Roman tradition can be traced back to sculptures erected in Turkey around 9500 B.C.

Tales of gods, goddesses, heroes, and monsters were told by firelight in nomads' camps, priestly temples, and echoing palaces. But today, most of them are forgotten. For the most part, they were never written down. Priests and itinerant poets memorized the myths word-for-word during apprenticeship and later were hired to recite them during long nights that were otherwise short on entertainment of any kind. But poets sometimes died without passing their tales on to apprentices, and over centuries many stories were lost along with their tellers.

Amazingly, the oral traditions of antiquity did manage to keep some myths alive over thousands of years and spread them across many lands. These were still being told in the warlord-ruled city-states that would later become the Greek Empire. The largest body of Greek mythology was built up around the nine-year-long Trojan War, which probably took place around 1200 B.C. The legends of this war focused on the roles the gods of Olympus played in starting the war and steering its outcome.

Most scholars believe that the stories of the Trojan War were pulled together into two huge epic poems about 500 years later. It is hard to believe that a single poet could memorize and recite either *The Iliad* or *The Odyssey* (as the two epics came to be known). Today, translated into

English and published in book form, *The Iliad* runs about 700 pages, and *The Odyssey,* 500 pages. It takes a long time to read them, never mind memorize them. But maybe the storytellers of that era didn't have to. For at about the same time—the early 8th century B.C.—Greek scholars redis-covered tablets containing a Phonecian alphabet that had been lost centuries earlier in the collapse of the Mycenaean civilization, around the same time as the Trojan War. They adapted it to their own language, and for the first time, it became possible to read and write Greek.

Soon after Greek emerged as a written language, someone known as Homer set about recording *The Iliad* and later *The Odyssey* on papyrus scrolls. With that act, the two epic poems became the very first European liter-ary works, and the gods and goddesses of ancient Greece became truly immortal.

Oddly enough, Homer never wrote down anything about himself, and to this day no one knows anything about who he was. He may have been as mythical as the gods and monsters he wrote about. For centuries, educated Greeks referred to the anonymous authors of all long written poems as "Homer," using the name as a synonym for "author." Modern scholars argue endlessly about "the Homer ques-tion," but most now concede that stylistic factors in both *The Iliad* and *The Odyssey* show each book—at least in the final versions—was written by a single person, and probably the same person.

The Parthenon in Athens.

The Greek gods formed the foundation of all religion in ancient Greece. Each of the Olympian gods had his or her own cult of priests, priestesses, and followers who came together to petition for the god's favor with ceremonies and animal sacrifices. Worship took place in temples dedicated to specific gods and goddesses. Some were modest, like roadside shrines to Hermes or forest clearings where early rituals honoring Dionysus were held. Others were the most impressive architectural accomplishments of the era, such as the Parthenon, located in the center of the Greek capital at Athens and dedicated to its patron goddess, Athena. With such tangible evidence of the presence and power of their gods, for centuries it never occurred to most people that the deities they worshipped might be mere campfire legends without physical existence. Unquestionably, in their minds, the Olympians were as real as wheat crops, thunderstorms, and war.

The same was true of the many fearsome monsters that populated *The Odyssey*. Most people, who never traveled more than 50 miles from home in their lifetimes, depended on storytellers for all their information about the world beyond the horizon, and why should a dragon, a giant cyclops, a woman with snakes for hair, or a robotic brass bull seem any less likely to exist than an elephant, a rhinoceros, an ostrich, or a gorilla?

The mythology of the ancient Greek gods and monsters was central to the culture of the time, and it carried over into other literature, especially the plays of Sophocles, Euripides, Aeschylus, and Aristophanes. A century or so later, the gods came under attack from the famed Greek philosopher Socrates and his followers, who rejected mythological explanations of the world. But Socrates's ideas were rejected by most Greeks of his time, and he was put on trial (for his political ideas, not his religious ones) and ultimately committed suicide.

As the gods of Mount Olympus continued to reign over Greece, big changes were happening 600 miles away on the far side of the Ionian Sea. Around 450 B.C., the newly formed Roman Republic began a huge military build-up designed at first to provide security against invasions by its neighbors. Soon it began invading and conquering other states on the Italian peninsula to form a united republic. Following an invasion by the Greek kingdom of Epirus, war broke out between Rome and Greece. The hostilities lasted for 72 years; in the end, Greece surrendered to Roman rule in 148 B.C.

The Gods Go Roman

The similarity between the mythologies of longtime rivals Greece and Rome is pronounced, and the Romans drew their religion much more from the Greeks than from any other people they conquered as their empire spread to the Middle East, the Germanic north, and the Gallic and British west. Greek gods, goddesses, heroes, and monsters were simply adopted wholesale by the Romans, who sometimes changed their names and perhaps small details of their lineages, other times not.

It may simply be that the Romans were less interested in religion than in religious ritual as a means of social organization. They erected monuments and temples to the gods and named planets, months, days, and celebrations for them, but Roman literature contained very little mythology. Consider Virgil's *Aeneid*, the greatest Roman epic poem, which like *The Iliad* and *The Odyssey* was set in the Trojan War and the years that followed. While a few gods and goddesses—including Juno (Hera), Jupiter (Zeus),

Neptune (Poseidon), and Venus (Aphrodite)—put in guest appearances, by the second half of the book the gods have all but faded from the scene. Roman readers much preferred history (the officially approved version) over tales of the supernatural. Most original Roman myths, such as those of the Sabine Women, Lucretia, Horatius, and Coriolanus, did not feature gods or monsters, though some legendary kings were claimed to be demigods, with goddesses as mothers (Roman gods didn't seem to play around with mortals as much at the Greek ones had).

A few of the Greek gods became more popular when they moved to Rome. As the god of war, Mars (Apollo) had countless temples and cults dedicated to him, and each Roman soldier would pay homage to his main temple before marching off to war. At the other extreme, Bacchus (Dionysus), the god of booze and debauchery, became a society hit as parties in his honor grew wilder and wilder. After the Senate passed a law against them, these orgies became more popular than ever.

Marble and bronze statues of the gods and goddesses (often copies from Greek originals) stood by the thousands throughout Rome. When the Roman Empire replaced the Roman Republic with the rise of Augustus Caesar as emperor in 27 B.C., statues of him and his successors were often placed on equal footing with those of the gods. This practice reached the height of absurdity with the insane Emperor Caligula. In A.D. 40, a year before he was assassinated by senate guards at the age of 29, Caligula made public appearances dressed up as various Olympian gods, introduced himself to foreign dignitaries as the "New Sun God," and ordered statues of gods throughout Rome to be decapitated and their heads replaced by marble busts of himself.

No wonder the people of a crumbling Rome started losing respect for the old-time religion. Facing deterioration on several fronts, including food shortages and civil war, Emperor Constantine ultimately decided to abandon the city to his rivals and move the seat of government to Byzantium, Turkey, which he renamed Nova Roma Constantinopolitana (the New Rome of Constantinople), capitol of the Eastern Roman Empire. He had earlier decreed a religious tolerance law that legalized the upstart religion of Christianity throughout the Roman Empire, and on his deathbed Constantine himself formally became a Christian.

Rome Goes Christian

As time passed, the new Roman Empire became the Holy Roman Empire, dominated by Roman Catholic clergy intent on erasing older religions from the face of the planet— especially the "pagans" who had persecuted their people for so long. Ancient temples fell into ruin and often became building materials for new churches. Statues of the gods and goddesses lay where they fell until the dust of time buried them. As for *The Iliad, The Odyssey, The Aeneid*, and all the other masterpieces of Greek and Roman literature, especially the ones filled with mythology, you might expect that the scrolls would be burned in bonfires—but they weren't. Not all of them, anyway.

That's the trouble with immortals. You can't kill them, you can only imprison them. For instance, the Olympians, upon defeating the Titans (who were also immortal), threw many of them into the pit of Tartarus, a place in the Underworld from which escape was impossible. The same thing happened to Greek and Roman scrolls. In those days, at the beginning of the Dark Ages, books were an extremely rare and valuable commodity, so they were not destroyed. Instead, they were hidden in the darkest, most secret corners of monastic libraries, where monks would take them out every century or so and copy their crumbling pages by hand. And there the old gods and goddesses, heroes and monsters remained, utterly forgotten by medieval civilization.

COMEBACK OF THE GODS

Throughout the Middle Ages, a slender book called the *Ilius Latina*—a much-abridged Latin version of *The Iliad*, about 10 percent the length of the original and censored to remove any supernatural content—was a standard textbook for the small minority of people who learned to read and write. This little glimpse into the ancient Greek world eventually spawned forgeries purporting to be histories of the Trojan War in several European languages. In 1473, one of them, the *Recuyell of the Historyes of Troye,* became the first book ever printed in English. As its popularity spread, it became faddish for British noblemen to concoct faux genealogies tracing their lineage back to characters in the Trojan War. Inevitably, copies of the original *Iliad* in its entirety leaked out, gods and all.

As the Renaissance began to flower across Europe, *The Iliad* and *The Odyssey* became some of the most popular best sellers of the time, and the immortals of Mount Olympus were on the loose once again. Shakespeare wrote plays about them, and painters and sculptors found in them a vast new body of subject matter with seemingly endless possibilities. Enthusiasm for all things classically Greek and Roman endured and grew, until by the 18th and 19th centuries no self-respecting mansion owner would be caught dead without reproductions of ancient statues of mythological beings in his gardens and foyer. Writers peppered their prose with references to the long-forgotten gods and monsters. Every truly educated aristocrat could quote passages from *The Iliad,* even though the text of the book, translated by stodgy scholarly types, was not always what you'd call exciting. The opening lines read:

Sing, O goddess, the anger of Achilles son of Peleus, that brought countless ills upon the Achaeans. Many a brave soul did it send hurrying down to Hades, and many a hero did it yield a prey to dogs and vultures, for so were the counsels of Jove fulfilled from the day on which the son of Atreus, king of men, and great Achilles, first fell out with one another. And which of the gods was it that set them on to quarrel? It was the son of Jove and Leto; for he was angry with the king and sent a pestilence upon the host to plague the people, because the son of Atreus had dishonored Chryses his priest . . .

It wasn't exactly edge-of-your-seat stuff by modern standards.

Heroes and Bananas

In the mid- to late 20th century, a new action- and adventure-loving America discovered an abundance of swords, sorcery, and sex hidden amid the verbiage of the ancient epic poems, with results that were often undignified and sometimes just plain silly. Marvel Comics brought many mythical characters into its pages, usually using their Roman names: Apollo, Ares, Hermes, Neptune, Venus, Zeus, and, of course, all-time favorite Hercules battled Gorgons, Titans, and new supervillains like Immortus and the Enchantress.

Hercules even faced off once with the Incredible Hulk. On television, mythical Greeks were staples in such shows as *Xena, Warrior Princess*.

But Greek and Roman mythology in the 20th century really belonged to the motion picture industry. From *Jason and the Argonauts* to *Clash of the Titans*, colorful costumes, swords, sorcery, and special effects provided all the elements for great (or not-so-great) action movies. As in comic books, Hercules (Greek name Hercules) was the favorite, beginning in 1959 with the low-budget Italian import *Hercules*, starring muscleman Steve Reeves, which became a surprise hit in the United States. It was the first of nine Hercules movies. Among them was *Hercules in New York*, which pitted the invincible superhero against cigar-chomping gangsters and crooked wrestling promoters. It was the first film appearance by Arnold Schwarzenegger (using the pseudonym Arnold Strong) and was later re-released under the title *Hercules Goes Bananas*.

But nothing else in pop culture has breathed new life into the myths of ancient Greece and Rome like the Percy Jackson & the Olympians and Heroes of Olympus books. While their popularity may pale in comparison to the unprecedented Harry Potter phenomenon, look at it this way: So far, the Percy Jackson books have sold more than 20 million copies worldwide. That's more than two-and-a-half times the entire population of ancient Greece at its peak, and 20 times the population of the city of Rome in antiquity, when it was the largest metropolis in the Western world. You could say that Zeus and his crew have never been as popular as they are today—thanks to a fictional, peculiar 12-year-old kid armed with a fountain pen.

Talk about immortality!

CHAPTER TWO

Meet the Twelve Olympians

AS EVERY READER of the Percy Jackson & the Olympians series knows, when they're not out on a quest, Percy and his fellow demigods at Camp Half-Blood live in cabins at a very unusual summer camp in upstate New York. There are 12 cabins, and they're named for the 12 Olympian gods of ancient Greece: Zeus, Poseidon, Demeter, Dionysus, Hermes, Ares, Athena, Apollo, Aphrodite, Hephaestus, Artemis, and Hera.

These are 12 most famous and powerful gods and goddesses in Greek and Roman mythology. They are known as the Olympians because they live on top of Mount Olympus, the highest mountain in Greece (elevation 9,570

Mount Olympus, the highest mountain in Greece and the mythological home of the gods.

feet). The mountain actually exists, and it's not particularly difficult to climb during the summer months when it's free of snow. Thousands of tourists make the ascent every year. Some ancient Greeks probably climbed it, too, and realized that no giant immortals actually lived there. At some point, mortals came to see the mountain itself as more of a metaphorical stairway to heaven, a symbol for a celestial home of the gods.

Although their genealogy was sometimes muddled and hard to trace, all the Olympians were related to each other, which did not stop them from seducing their own siblings, as well as having illicit affairs of every description with gods and mortals alike—not to mention drinking, gambling, stealing livestock, and devouring their own children. Parents of younger readers of the series, or, for that matter, of such great literary works as Homer's *Iliad* and *Odyssey*, would likely disapprove of such goings-on (so please don't tell them).

These gods were clearly less concerned about moral-
ity than divinities of newer religions tend to be. In fact, they
didn't seem to take much interest at all in the well-being
of humans, except as playthings. Some of the Olympian
gods liked to start wars simply for entertainment, seemingly oblivious to the massive carnage that resulted when
thousands of mortal soldiers hacked each other to pieces
with swords. They viewed human beings as something like
domesticated animals who could talk, and they graciously
accepted the sacrifices of food and treasures that humans
left at their temples in hope that the gods would grant them
good fortune, victory in battle, smooth sailing, rain for
their crops, or any of the other boons that were beyond the
power of mere mortals. Whether the gods actually granted
these things or only promised them is hard to say.

What the gods did do in their heyday was to make
mortals feel that they had greater understanding of the
world's great forces—such as thunder and lightning, storms
at sea, fire, agricultural crops, and the four seasons, as well
as abstractions like wisdom, art, and sensuality—by giving
them personalities that humans could relate to. Even today,
psychoanalysts who follow the teachings of Carl Jung study
the central Greek gods as "archetypes" that help us identify
the basic traits common to all human beings around the
world and throughout the ages.

With that in mind, let's take a closer look at each of
the twelve Olympian gods of Greece and Rome.

APHRODITE
ROMAN NAME: VENUS

SPHERE OF INFLUENCE: Love, beauty, pleasure, and sexuality. In early Rome, Venus had been a goddess of vegetation and the patroness of gardens and vineyards. It was only after the Romans came into contact with the Greeks that she assumed many of the characteristics of the goddess Aphrodite.

SYMBOLS: Seashell, dolphin, rose, mirror, swan.

ORIGIN: Among numerous versions of Aphrodite's origin, the most commonly told is that she was born from sea foam that formed when the titan Kronos castrated his father, Uranus, god of the sky, at the request of his mother, Gaea, and then threw his testicles into the sea. Aphrodite came into the world full-grown and was of an earlier generation than Zeus, the ruler of the gods.

FAMILY TIES: Hoping to prevent the sensual Aphrodite from sparking violent scandals on Mount Olympus, Zeus ordered her to marry the stodgy god of blacksmiths, Hephaestus (Roman name Vulcan). Nevertheless, she had affairs with many other Olympians, including the great love of her life, Ares, the war god, as well as Poseidon, Hermes, and Dionysus, among others. She bore at least 15 children and also gave birth to several half-humans, the most famous being Aeneas, a hero in Homer's *Iliad* and Virgil's *Aenead*, who survived the conquest of Troy and went on to found

Rome. Aphrodite's motherly love for Aeneas inspired her to take a more active role in the Trojan War than any other god except Ares. In Roman mythology, Venus and Mars (Ares) were also the parents of Cupid (counterpart of the Greek primordial god Eros), the flirtatious and fickle spirit of romantic love.

MYTHS AND LEGENDS: Aphrodite took pity on the infant Adonis, whose mother could not care for him because she had been turned into a tree. Aphrodite later handed him over to Persephone, queen of the Underworld, who raised him. When Aphrodite visited the land of the dead again many years later, she found that Adonis had grown into a beautiful youth and wanted him back as her lover. Zeus decreed that each goddess would care for him for part of the year. One of the most complex figures in Greco-Roman mythology, Adonis was based on earlier figures symbolizing nature's birth-death-rebirth cycle and the beauty of youth in Syrian, Egyptian, and Hebrew myths; today he is a central archetype in Jungian psychology.

TEMPLES OF WORSHIP: The main temple to the cult of Aphrodite was located in Paphos on the island of Cyprus. Said to be the spot where the goddess was born from sea foam, it had earlier been the site of temples dedicated to Assyrian and Babylonian fertility goddesses.

Artistic Depictions: Aphrodite has been a favorite artists' subject throughout history. She is always depicted as a beautiful woman, usually naked, and seated within a scallop shell. Her symbols include a dove, an apple, and a mirror. She is the goddess not only of love, but also of beauty and grace, and has the power to grant beauty and invincible charms to others. The *Aphrodite of Milos*, also known as the *Venus de Milo* (ca. 130–100 B.C.), one of the best-known ancient Greek sculptures, was rediscovered by a Greek peasant in the ancient city of Milos in 1820. Famously armless, it is exhibited at the Louvre in Paris. *The Birth of Venus*, a famous painting by Italian Renaissance artist Sandro Botticelli, shows Aphrodite rising out of the sea in a giant scallop shell surrounded by cherubs and nymphs. It can be seen in the Uffizi Gallery in Florence, Italy.

APOLLO
ROMAN NAME: APOLLO

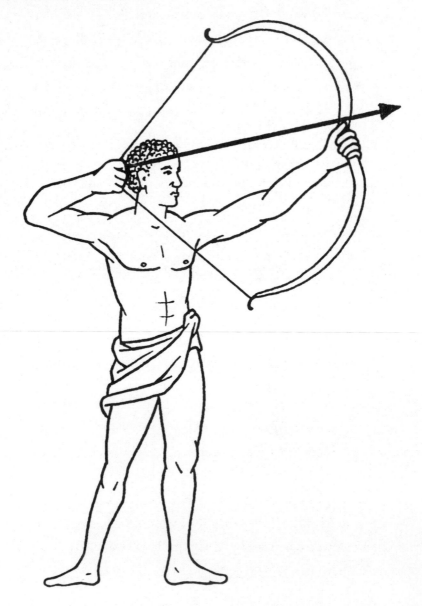

Sphere of Influence: Music, poetry, education, healing, archery, and the protection of the young.

Symbols: Lyre, laurel wreath, bow and arrows.

Origin: Zeus, in a dalliance with the Titan goddess Leto, conceived Apollo and his twin sister, Artemis. Out of jealousy, Zeus's wife Hera banished Leto from all the lands on earth, so she gave birth to the twins on the floating island of Delos. Upon his birth, Apollo was fed ambrosia and nectar, and when he tasted the divine food he declared that from then on he would tell everyone the will of Zeus through prophecy. Later, worshippers of Apollo and Artemis flocked to his oracle at Delos in boats, and in gratitude for the wealth of offerings they brought, the people of Delos affixed the island to the sea bottom with massive pillars, making it easier to find. Leto remained banished on the island and played no further role in Greek or Roman mythology.

Family Ties: Apollo never married but had many lovers, both female and male, and seems to have been especially partial to wood and water nymphs. One nymph, Daphne, became a casualty of a rivalry between Apollo and Cupid, who shot Apollo with a golden arrow that caused him to fall in love with her, but then shot Daphne with a lead one so that she was repulsed by him. Apollo pursued her, but to no avail, until she begged for help from her father, a river god, who changed her into a laurel tree; leaves and branches from laurel trees are important in oracle ceremonies. Apollo also sired a son with Hecuba, wife of the king of Troy. The son's story would be retold thousands of years later in Shakespeare's tragedy *Troilus and Cressida*. Apollo is usually credited with conceiving Orpheus, the greatest musician of ancient times, with Calliope, the muse who inspired Homer to write *The Iliad* and *The Odyssey*. Apollo's same-sex lovers included Spartan prince Hyacinth, whose untimely death he commemorated by naming a species of flower after him, and Cypress, whom Apollo transformed into the "weeping" tree of the same name after Cypress accidentally killed his pet deer.

The remains of the temple of Apollo at Delphi.

MYTHS AND LEGENDS: Apollo replaced the original Titan god of the sun, Helios, and thus came to be known as the light-bringer. Although Apollo is usually associated with art, beauty, and radiance, he had a dark side, too. Heart attacks and other sudden deaths were blamed on him, and he helped the Trojans in their war against the Greeks by sending plague-tipped arrows against the Greek armies.

TEMPLES OF WORSHIP: The two most important sites dedicated to the cult of Apollo were the temple at his birthplace on the island of Delos and the famous oracle shrine at Delphi. Apollo also reigned over about a dozen other shrines across the eastern Mediterranean region where kings, generals, and priests came to receive prophecies about the future.

ARTISTIC DEPICTIONS: Apollo was a favorite subject for the portrayal of the perfect male form, both in ancient times and during the Renaissance. Some of the best-known statues of him are the life-size sculptures at the Archaeological Museum of Piraeus in Athens, the Vatican Museum in Rome, the Louvre in Paris, and the State Hermitage Museum in St. Petersburg, Russia, not to mention the audio-animatronic version at Caesars Palace in Las Vegas.

※ ※ ※ ※

ARES
ROMAN NAME: MARS

SPHERE OF INFLUENCE: War, battle lust, civil order, physical valor, and courage.

SYMBOLS: Chariot, spear, helmet, boar (Greek), wolf (Roman).

ORIGIN: In Greek mythology, Ares was the son of Zeus and his wife Hera; in the Roman version, Mars was the son of Hera alone, conceived through the use of a magic flower. Ares was regarded with ambivalence by the Greeks, both godly and mortal. Except for his bloodthirsty role in the Trojan War as recounted in Homer's *Iliad*, Ares appeared in Greek mythology mainly as a raunchy seducer of women, the tales often involving rape. Later, he was absorbed into the Roman pantheon of gods under the name Mars and gained great respect as the god of the military.

FAMILY TIES: Ares's most enduring love affair was with Aphrodite, the goddess of love. Although she was married to another god, Aphrodite's long-standing fascination with bad-boy Ares resulted in five godly offspring, some of whom were lovers and others, fighters. Of the three who reflected aspects of Aphrodite's personality, Eros (known to the Romans as Cupid) was the god of sexual love; his brother

Anteros ruled over requited love and marriage; and their sister, Harmonia, represented peace and harmony. But the other two sons, Phobos and Deimos, accompanied Ares into war as disembodied spirits personifying fear and terror. Although the planet Mars bears the war god's Roman name, the Martian moons, Phobos and Deimos, are known by their Greek names. In Roman mythology, Mars is sometimes credited with being the father of Romulus and Remus, the feral twins who founded Rome. (Other versions of the legend identify Aeneas or Hercules as the twins' father.)

MYTHS AND LEGENDS: Ares and Athena found themselves on opposite sides in the Trojan War, and the war god was once wounded by the goddess of wisdom and justice. The two met more than once on the battlefield outside the gates of Troy, the last time being when Ares tried to destroy the Trojan Horse and Athena sought to defend it. The fight between them was called off when Zeus ordered all the gods and goddesses off the field of battle.

In his Roman manifestation, Mars spent a good deal of time in conflict with his fellow gods. He killed one of Neptune's sons for raping one of his daughters and as a result was brought to trial before his fellow gods on a charge of murder. Unlike the other gods and goddesses associated with war, Mars loved war for its own sake. He personified the chaos of war—its noise, confusion, and horrors. He delighted in the slaughter of men and the destruction of towns and cities and would sometimes even take both sides in a battle, first helping one army and then the other. This less-than-heroic trait made him a disappointment to his mother, Juno.

TEMPLES OF WORSHIP: No major temple in Greece was dedicated to Ares, though sacrifices to him were held at the Phoebaeum near Sparta. As Mars, he had many temples throughout the Roman Empire, from Turkey and Greece to Britain. The most important was at Porta Capena in Rome, where armies gathered before going to war.

ARTISTIC DEPICTIONS: Ares or Mars is often depicted nude except for his weapons of war. Perhaps the most familiar such image is a marble statue known as the *Ares Borghese*, which was originally erected in the Forum in Athens; a Roman copy of it now resides in the Louvre in Paris. A fresco of Mars from Pompeii, also nude except for his helmet, spear, and shield, is in the Museo Archaeologico Nazionale in Naples, Italy. The *Ares Ludovisi*, a Roman copy of a 5th century B.C. Greek marble sculpture, can be seen at the National Museum of the Terme in Rome.

❋ ❋ ❋ ❋

ARTEMIS
ROMAN NAME: DIANA

Sphere of Influence: Moon, wild forests, hunting, and midwifery.

Symbols: Moon, bow and arrows, hunting hound, deer.

Origin: Artemis was the twin sister of Apollo, conceived by Zeus with the Titan goddess Leto. The twins were born on a floating island after Zeus's wife, Hera, banished Leto from all the lands of the earth.

Family Ties: At age three, Zeus granted Artemis's wish that she would always remain a virgin. She never married but had numerous male hunting companions at different times, including her one great love, the heroic hunter Orion, who was murdered—according to some versions of the legend—to protect Artemis's chastity. She had no children but was usually attended by wood nymphs and accompanied by a pack of 13 dogs, a gift from the goat-god Pan.

Myths and Legends: Like her brother, Artemis sided with the Trojans in their war with the Greeks and did her best to prevent the Greek fleet from even setting sail. Agamemnon, king of Mycenai, had offended her by claiming to be a better hunter, so she created huge storm winds that stopped his ships from leaving port. To appease the goddess, the king was forced to sacrifice his own daughter, and only after doing so did the winds die down, allowing the Greek fleet to set sail. Later she helped heal the Trojan hero Aeneas and actually came to blows with Hera, who sided with the Greeks in the conflict. Like her brother, Apollo, Artemis had the power to bring sudden death and disease, but she only targeted women and girls, while he went after men and boys. She required her followers to share her oath of chastity, and woe betide any who broke that oath: Her punishments were swift and mean. When one of her handmaiden wood nymphs, Callisto, was seduced by Zeus and tried to hide her pregnancy, Artemis turned the unfortunate woman into a bear and cast her into the heavens, where she became the constellation Ursa Major. Today, Diana is worshipped in the United States by a feminist branch of the Wicca religious movement.

Temples of Worship: In Greece, Artemis was a favorite cult figure, and many people offered sacrifices to her for good luck in hunting. Important temples, in addition to the one at her birthplace on Delos, included one at Brauron in Attica, adolescent girls were sent to her temple for one year before they could marry. Romans also built many temples and sanctuaries to Diana from Portugal to Jordan. Her temple at Ephesus was considered one of the Seven Wonders of the Ancient World.

Artistic Depictions: Artemis or Diana has usually been depicted as a girl dressed in a knee-length garment, carrying

The sanctuary of Artemis at Brauron (modern-day Vravrona).

a hunting bow and a quiver of arrows, though in her role as moon goddess she wears a long dress instead. She has been one of the most popular immortal subjects for both classical and contemporary artists. One of the best-known classical statues of her is the *Diana of Versailles,* a Roman copy of a 4th century B.C. Greek statue, which can be seen in the Louvre in Paris. In more recent times, she has been painted by such masters as Titian, Rubens, and Rembrandt. A huge, stylized bronze statue of her by 19th-century Irish-American sculptor Augustus Saint-Gaudens dominates the atrium in New York City's Metropolitan Museum of Art.

❀ ❀ ❀ ❀

ATHENA
ROMAN NAME: MINERVA

Sphere of Influence: Wise counsel, philosophy, magic, military strategy, heroic endeavors, weaving, and pottery.

Symbols: Olive branch, serpent owl, shepherd's staff, lance, shield with Medusa-head emblem.

Origin: Under various names, Athena was worshipped throughout the Middle East, Egypt, Crete, and North Africa for thousands of years, so she arrived in ancient Greece bringing many legends with her, including one of the strangest origin stories ever. Supposedly she was conceived parthenogenetically—that is, without sexual intercourse—by Metis, the Titan goddess of wisdom and devious thought. When Zeus and his brothers seized power from the Titans, a prophecy predicted that a child of Metis would become greater than Zeus. To prevent this, Zeus devoured Metis, not knowing that she was already pregnant with Athena. Then Zeus suffered headaches so terrible that he asked one of his fellow gods to release the pain by splitting his skull with an axe, whereupon Athena emerged full-grown and dressed for battle.

Family Ties: Athena remained a virgin and never took a husband or lover. She had no children.

Myths and Legends: Athena was known for her association with scientific inventions. She is said to have inspired the invention of the trumpet, the chariot, numbers, and navigation. Aside from assisting with those inventions, she was also believed to have given men the means and the instruments for using them. So not only did she give them flint and stone, she also gave them the idea of striking the two together.

As the goddess of wise counsel, she was also the patron divinity of the apparatus of government and maintaining the authority of the law, justice, and order in the courts and assemblies of the people. In Greece, she inspired the concept of democracy. In Rome, as the goddess Minerva, her skills as a military strategist became more important. Unlike Mars, the god of war, Minerva did not love war but recognized the need for it when the state was under attack. She encouraged men to seek a peaceful resolution to armed conflict first and only resort to war when there was no other choice.

In contemporary American literature, Athena is the mother (again by virgin birth) of demigoddess Annabeth, a central character in Rick Riordan's Percy Jackson & the Olympians and Heroes of Olympus series.

TEMPLES OF WORSHIP: Athena was the patron goddess of Athens, Greece, where the most magnificent temple in the city, the Parthenon, was built in her honor. It is considered the finest achievement of ancient Greek architecture.

Artistic Depictions: Athena is usually depicted as thoughtful, earnest, and majestic, slender but strong, wearing an ornate helmet, a sleeveless tunic, and a cloak. In both Greece and Rome, statues of her were often monumentally large, such as the 100-foot-tall 5th century B.C. gold and ivory statue that stood in the Parthenon in Athens. Although the original statue was destroyed, a smaller-scale Roman replica stands in Athens's National Archaeological Museum. Another copy, 42 feet tall, stands in the full-size concrete replica of the Parthenon that serves as a public art museum in Centennial Park in Nashville, Tennessee. Other large statues depicting the Roman goddess Minerva are found around the world in cities as diverse as Brooklyn, New York; Portland, Maine; Minneapolis, Minnesota; Glasgow, Scotland; Guadalajara, Mexico; and Bangalore, India.

�֎ ✖ ✖ ✖

DEMETER
ROMAN NAME: CERES

Sphere of Influence: Crops, harvests, fertility, the seasons, and sanctity of marriage.

Symbols: Cornucopia, wheat, torch, lion, poppy.

Origin: Demeter was a child of the Titans Kronos and Rhea, as were several other Olympian gods, including Hera, Hades, Zeus, and Poseidon. Because Gaea had predicted that Kronos would be overthrown by one of his offspring, he took the precaution of eating his children at birth. Long afterward, Kronos was given a drug that caused him to vomit up his children, who then went to war against the Titans and overthrew them.

Family Ties: Demeter did not marry but had many affairs with gods, men, and even horses. With her brother Zeus, she conceived Persephone, who would become the queen of the Underworld, and also, according to some versions of the legend, Dionysus, the god of wine.

Another of Demeter's brothers, Poseidon, in the guise of a stallion, forced himself on her and sired the goddess Despoine as well as the immortal horse Areion, who would become Heracles's steed.

Myths and Legends: When her daughter Persephone was abducted by Hades, lord of the Underworld, with Zeus's consent, Demeter not only left the home of the gods but withdrew fertility from the earth, causing great famine among men. To end the famine, Zeus and Hades agreed to let Persephone leave the Underworld for part of the year, giving rise to the seasons. During her search for Persephone, Demeter was welcomed into the court of Celeus, the king of the Greek city-state of Eleusis, who asked her to nurse and care for his two sons. In thanks for his hospitality, Demeter offered to make one of the sons a god, but her ritual failed when it was interrupted by the child's mother. Instead, Demeter decided to teach the other son, Triptolemus, the secrets of growing crops, and he traveled throughout Greece in a flying chariot, sharing his knowledge of agriculture.

TEMPLES OF WORSHIP: Most temples to Demeter or Ceres were located in rural areas since their purpose was to offer sacrifices for bountiful crop harvests. For this reason, they were usually modest structures, often made of wood, and few have survived.

ARTISTIC DEPICTIONS: Demeter or Ceres was often depicted as a mature woman crowned and holding sheaves of wheat and a torch. This is only fitting for the goddess who was not only considered the goddess of fertility for the fields but for women as well. The mother goddess of the ancient world, she was more matronly than many of the goddesses. In Imperial Rome, following agricultural reforms in the 1st century A.D., Ceres was traditionally represented on the back of coins as a reminder that the emperor and the gods were equal partners in grain production. Classical Roman marble statues of Ceres can be found in the Vatican Museum in Rome and the National Museum of Roman Art in Mérida, Spain.

※ ※ ※ ※

DIONYSUS
ROMAN NAME: BACCHUS

Sphere of Influence: Wine, theatre, intoxication, and ecstatic madness.

Symbols: Grapevine, leopard skin.

Origin: Dionysus, the child of Zeus and Semele—a mortal who is variously described as a priestess of Zeus or a princess of Thebes—was born in almost as unusual a manner as his half-sister Athena. Hera, being jealous of any of her husband's lovers, cast doubt on whether the person who impregnated Semele was actually a god and so tricked her into begging Zeus to reveal himself to her in his godly form. Since mortals who beheld gods in their true form often died of fright, Semele caught fire. As she died, she gave birth three months early, and the infant Dionysus would not have survived if he hadn't been saved from the fire by Hermes and sewn up into Zeus's thigh, where he grew to full term. The fact that he was "born" twice, the second time from Zeus himself, may explain why he became an immortal god instead of a mere demigod.

Family Ties: To keep Dionysus safe from Hera's wrath, according to a popular version of the legend, Zeus changed him into a ram and gave him over to be raised by rain nymphs in a distant land. There he learned how to grow grapes and make wine from them. He traveled the world teaching these skills and ultimately returned to Greece, where he found himself at the center of a controversy over whether mortals should be allowed to drink alcoholic beverages. He married Ariadne, a daughter of the king of Crete, who gave him 11 children. Party animal that he was, Dionysus also bedded dozens of other women, both goddesses and mortals (including Aphrodite), and sired many children.

MYTHS AND LEGENDS: Dionysus, like Apollo, possessed the power to reveal the future through oracles and to heal. In Greece, his worship developed into a cult known as the Dionysian Mysteries, in which wine was used to induce prophetic visions. In Rome, where he was known as Bacchus, he was often celebrated in drunken gatherings called "bacchanalia." His cult became wildly popular but no less

A Roman bacchanalia.

controversial than it had been in Greece. At first the bacchanalia were for women only and took place once a year, lasting two days and nights. But soon men began joining in, too, turning them into orgies, and instead of an annual celebration, they came to be held five times a month. Bacchanalia were held in secret, and besides drunken debauchery their secrecy also made them an ideal place to hatch conspiracies and criminal plots. They were ultimately banned by the Roman Senate in 186 B.C., which made them even more secret but no less popular, and bacchanalia continued to be held in Rome and other parts of the empire for centuries. At the same time, Bacchus was officially removed from the list of Olympian gods and replaced by Vesta (Greek name Hestia), purportedly to achieve a gender balance on Mount Olympus.

TEMPLES OF WORSHIP: Early rituals were held in the woods. Later temples dedicated to him were often built as representations of the forest—circles of columns with no roofs—and became amphitheaters used to perform plays. Temples and theaters dedicated to Dionysus sprang up all over the Mediterranean world. Examples can still be seen in Naxos, Greece, and in Pergamum, Turkey.

ARTISTIC DEPICTIONS: Dionysus was depicted most often as a rather pretty and effeminate long-haired youth carrying a pine cone–tipped staff and holding a drinking cup, sometimes accompanied by a leopard and a troop of fauns and *mainades*, the name given to his female devotees. In ancient times, Bacchus's image was often painted on cups used for drinking wine. In more recent times, he has been a favorite subject of many visual artists, from Michelangelo and Caravaggio to Walt Disney.

❊ ❊ ❊ ❊

HEPHAESTUS
ROMAN NAME: VULCAN

Sphere of Influence: Metalworking, fire, building, sculpture, and volcanoes.

Symbols: Hammer, anvil.

Origin: Hephaestus was one of the two children of Zeus and Hera, according to most versions of the myth, though some say Hera conceived him alone by parthenogenesis. When she saw that he had been born lame, his mother threw him from Mount Olympus because his appearance brought shame to her as queen of heaven. He was saved from death by Thetis, a goddess of the sea, but the fall left him even more crippled. He returned to Mount Olympus to make thrones of gold for the other gods.

Family Ties: Hephaestus was wed to Aphrodite in a marriage arranged by Zeus, but there seems to have been no love lost between them. When Aphrodite embarked on her longtime affair with Ares, Hephaestus wanted to present Zeus with proof of her infidelity. He made a gossamer-thin metal net, set it to snare anyone in his bed, and then told Aphrodite he had to go out of town. She sent word to Ares that he should come join her. When he did, they were caught in the net in a compromising position and held there for all the gods to see. Although Hephaestus and Aphrodite had no children together, he sired many lesser gods and goddesses by others and later, in his Roman version, also fathered monsters such as the fire-breathing, man-eating monster Cacus, who was ultimately conquered by Heracles.

MYTHS AND LEGENDS: It was Hephaestus, under the guidance of Zeus, who actually made the physical body of Pandora and then bound the Titan Prometheus to the rock after he had stolen fire and given it to men. However, he was most famously known for his metal works, especially his armor. Not only did he fashion the armor worn by the Trojan heroes Aeneas and Memnon, showing he didn't play any favorites in the war, he also made armor for the Greek warriors Achilles and Diomedes. He also made armor and a shield for Heracles. In an earlier Roman legend, after the war with the giants and the defeat of Typhon, the "father of all monsters" who was buried under Mount Etna, Vulcan's

The temple of Hephaestus in Athens.

anvil was placed on the giant's neck to make sure he was held permanently in place.

TEMPLES OF WORSHIP: The forge where Hephaestus made all his creations, including the armor for gods and heroes, was located beneath the volcanic Mount Etna on present-day Sicily, an Italian island first colonized by the Greeks. Later the Romans renamed him Vulcan and celebrated him in the Vulcanalia festival on August 23 each year by lighting fires all along the Tiber River and roasting live fish over them. The Romans kept his temples either outside or on the outskirts of their cities due to the risk of fire. The 2,400-year-old temple of Hephaestus in the Agora of Athens is the best-preserved ancient temple in Greece.

ARTISTIC DEPICTIONS: Unlike the other gods, Hephaestus was not known for his looks or his strength. Instead, he was usually shown riding on the back of a donkey and carrying the hammer and tongs of a blacksmith.

❈ ❈ ❈ ❈

HERA
ROMAN NAME: JUNO

Sphere of Influence: Heavens, sky, women, marriage, and family.

Symbols: Crown, lotus-tipped staff, hawk, cuckoo, lion.

Origin: Hera was among the Olympian gods who were children of the Titans Kronos and Rhea, along with her brothers Poseidon, Hades, and Zeus, and sisters Hestia and Demeter, as well as Chiron the centaur. Kronos ate his offspring at birth to protect himself from a prophecy that they would overthrow him—which they did long afterward when he was forced to vomit them up.

Family Ties: Hera married her brother Zeus and reigned by his side. She gave birth to Ares, the god of war, and several lesser gods and goddesses by Zeus. Some myths of Hera claim she was a lifelong virgin who conceived Zeus's children by beating her hand on the ground. The god Hephaestus, especially, was widely viewed as being Hera's child alone, without Zeus's participation. Unlike most other gods, Hera was faithful to her husband and did not take lovers, but she was jealous and vindictive about Zeus's many affairs and often meted out horrifying punishments against the women he dallied with.

Myths and Legends: Much of Hera's time and energy was devoted to persecuting both the children of her husband's affairs and the women he had the affairs with. As the goddess of marriage, she took each of these affairs as a personal insult. But she did have her favorites among heroes, especially Jason, and she did her best to assist him and his crew of Argonauts in their quest for a treasure known as the Golden Fleece.

Aside from her role in legends about the fates of Zeus's lovers, two other stories about Hera stand out. She especially hated one of Zeus's illegitimate demigod sons from birth, even when the boy was renamed Heracles in her honor. After he married, Hera drove Heracles insane, causing him to murder his own children. As punishment, Heracles was sentenced to perform twelve "labors"—increasingly dangerous and difficult tasks—which he succeeded in doing. Some versions of the legend hold that Hera later forgave Heracles and declared him the greatest of Greece's Olympian heroes (in fact, the word "hero" probably derived from the name Hera) and made him an immortal god after his human death.

One of the most important stories associated with Hera was the Judgement of Paris. When the goddess of discord, Eris to the Greeks, was refused entry to a wedding, she left behind a golden apple addressed "To the Fairest." Hera, Aphrodite, and Athena all laid claim to the title and the apple. When Zeus was asked to judge between them, he wisely declined and ordered Hermes to lead the three goddesses to Paris, a prince of Troy, to make the decision.

Aphrodite bribed Paris, promising him the hand of Helen, the world's most beautiful mortal woman. This not only started the Trojan War but, when Aphrodite favored the Trojans and Hera, the Greeks, it led to most of the Olympian gods taking one side or the other, making the Trojan War a pivotal event in Greek and Roman mythology.

TEMPLES OF WORSHIP: Hera personified the Mother Goddess worshipped by pre-Greek matriarchal societies. As such, temples dedicated to her were among the oldest and largest in the ancient world, including several that once stood as Samos, where cults from such distant lands as Babylon, Syria, Egypt, and Persia came to worship. The Temple of Hera at Olympia, Greece was destroyed by an earthquake around A.D. 300, but its site is still used for the ceremonial lighting of the Olympic torch in modern times.

ARTISTIC DEPICTIONS: Classical Greek and Roman statues of Hera or Juno abound throughout the Mediterranean world. Among the most familiar images of her that has survived is the *Hera Campana,* a Roman copy from a lost Greek sculpture, which stands in the Louvre in Paris. In 2006, a headless statue of Hera dating back 2,200 years was discovered sealed inside a city wall at Mount Olympus, the tallest mountain in Greece and the mythological home of the gods.

❈ ❈ ❈ ❈

HERMES
ROMAN NAME: MERCURY

SPHERE OF INFLUENCE: Communications, oratory, diplomacy, literature, trickery, thievery, travel, borders, athletics, and inventions.

SYMBOLS: Winged sandals, winged hat, caduceus (staff entwined by snakes), lyre, tortoise, rooster.

ORIGIN: Hermes was the son of Zeus by a mountain nymph named Maia, one of the daughters of the Titan Atlas. He was born in a cave in the Greek state of Arcadia, but as soon as his mother fell asleep, he snuck away and stole a herd of immortal oxen from Apollo. To calm Apollo's anger, he played music on a lyre he had invented from a tortoise shell, and Apollo, as the god of music, traded his cattle for the instrument. Hermes was then invited to join the pantheon of gods on Mount Olympus, but he spent most of his time traveling the earth. He even discovered the route to the Underworld, becoming the guide for others who tried to visit Hades's realm and return alive.

FAMILY TIES: Hermes had an eye for the ladies—especially nymphs—and is credited with siring at least 42 immortal children. Some of them were strange in appearance, such as the half-man, half-goat god Pan and the half-male, half-female Hermaphroditus, born of Aphrodite.

Myths and Legends: Hermes was the most "mercurial" of the ancient gods—hard to pin down. Like other gods, he was adapted by the Greeks and later the Romans from deities worshipped by earlier cultures. But as a trickster, a bringer of good luck, and a world traveler he came to represent a wide variety of traits that did not easily fit into the court of the Olympians. Besides travelers, he protected

smugglers, thieves, and prostitutes. He invented the alphabet and grammar, enabled communication across distances in a time before literacy, and brought dreams to sleeping mortals, but he was also as likely to lie as to tell the truth. He combined the qualities of older gods from as far away as Germany, Ireland, Spain, the Middle East, and North Africa, and would have

The caduceus is symbol of Hermes.

been perfectly at home in the role of Coyote, the trickster of Native American folklore.

Temples of Worship: According to historians, roadside shrines to Hermes or Mercury were very common in Greece and throughout the Roman Empire, though few have been preserved. As the patron of athletics, statues of him were also placed in gymnasiums, where he was often shown as having prodigiously large genitals.

Artistic Depictions: Hermes or Mercury is depicted as either a handsome and athletic youth or an older bearded man, but he is always shown wearing his winged sandals and winged hat, and of course carrying the caduceus, the herald's staff with a pair of entwined snakes wrapped around it. A Roman marble copy of a Greek bronze sculpture, on display in the Louvre in Paris, shows him putting on his flying sandals.

POSEIDON
ROMAN NAME: NEPTUNE

Sphere of Influence: Seas, rivers, earthquakes, floods, drought, and horses.

Symbols: Trident, dolphin.

Origin: Poseidon was one of the sons of Titans Kronos and Rhea. Some versions of the legend say that he was devoured by Kronos and later freed by his youngest brother, Zeus, while others say he was hidden by Rhea, who gave Kronos a young horse to eat in his place, and raised on the island of Rhodes by Telchines, fish children with fins instead of hands. In any case, he came back to help his brothers overthrow the Titans and divide the realms of the world between themselves.

Family Ties: Poseidon's original wife was Amphitrite, a sea goddess, but she faded out of mythology over the centuries as more and more tales described the god's dalliances with other women and occasionally men. Poseidon had more immortal and semimortal offspring than any other Greek god. While most of them were so obscure that only Classics professors would recognize their names, an exception was Pegasus, the winged horse, whom he conceived with the Gorgon Medusa. Other strange children of Poseidon included Antaeus, his child with Gaea, who liked to wrestle people to death and then decorate his temple to his father with their skulls; Charybdis, the sea monster/whirlpool that would drag ships to the bottom of the sea in the straits of Messina; Polyphemus, the man-eating Cyclops giant who attacked Odysseus (Roman name Ulysses) and his crew; and Laistrygon, the king of the man-eating giant tribe that took their name from him the Laistrygones. He also had nicer children, such as Theseus, the Athenian hero who slew the Minotaur, and Bellerophon, who tamed Pegasus and defeated the Chimera. With Amphitrite (Roman name Salacia), he had four children, chief among whom was Triton, god of the depths of the seas. And then, of course, there's Percy Jackson....

Temple to Poseidon at Cape Sounion.

MYTHS AND LEGENDS: As the god who controlled the power of the seas, Poseidon often played a key role in the outcome of naval battles in *The Iliad* and harrowing sea adventures in *The Odyssey*. He engaged in a legendary competition with Athena for dominion over the city of Athens, the Greek capital and major seaport. This competition is depicted in the elaborate frieze that decorates the front of the Parthenon, the city's magnificent temple to Athena.

TEMPLES OF WORSHIP: Because they were virtually always built along the seacoast, many temples to Poseidon have weathered badly over the centuries. The best-preserved is at Cape Sounion, a popular day-trip from Athens for modern tourists who come to watch the sun set over the Aegean Sea from its spectacular clifftop setting.

ARTISTIC DEPICTIONS: Poseidon is typically portrayed in sculptures as a powerful, mature man with a long, curly beard, holding a trident. The trident itself, which was usually crafted of bronze because it was too delicate to carve from marble, is often missing from the statues that survive, such as the famous *Poseidon of Milos* that now stands in the National Archaeological Museum of Athens.

✳✳✳✳

ZEUS
ROMAN NAME: JUPITER

Sphere of Influence: Sky, thunder, weather, law, order, fate, and kingship.

Symbols: Lightning bolt, royal scepter, eagle

Origin: Zeus was the youngest son of Kronos and Rhea, Titans who ruled the earth at the dawn of time. A prophecy foretold that Kronos would be overthrown by his own son, so the Titan sought to avoid this fate by eating his children as soon as Rhea gave birth to them. But Rhea gave birth to Zeus while away from home in Crete. She left him in a cave on Mount Ida in Crete, where different versions of the legend have him being raised by earth goddess Gaea, or by one of various nymphs, or by shepherds, or by a female goat. When he grew up, Zeus returned and forced Kronos to disgorge his siblings, who then overthrew the Titan as predicted, divided the world among themselves, and set up a new order of gods and goddesses on Mount Olympus.

Family Ties: Zeus's wife Hera gave him five children, though some accounts claim three of them were conceived parthenogenetically, without fertilization by a male. Zeus was notorious for his many affairs with goddesses, Titans, nymphs, and mortal women, and whenever there wasn't a war going on, it seemed that the main focus of Greek and Roman mythology was Zeus's lust and deception—and Hera's jealousy and revenge. He often assumed the form

of an animal to accomplish his seduction, most famously a
swan or a bull, for if a mortal woman looked at Zeus in his
true form she would catch fire and die. He fathered quite a
few children—demigods, gods, and monsters alike. Artemis,
the goddess of the hunt, was his daughter by the Titan
Leto; Hermes, the messenger god, was his son by Maia,
a daughter of Atlas.

MYTHS AND LEGENDS: Zeus was the highest authority
on Mount Olympus, the god to whom all the other gods
answered, and much of his role was to hand down decrees
that would avoid or resolve disputes among the other gods.
He also was in charge of welcoming guests and showing
hospitality to strangers. He received oaths from humans and
made sure they kept them. All-seeing, all-knowing, and all-
powerful, he could see what was happening everywhere,
to everyone. (Whether he did anything about it is another
matter.) Most of all, Zeus's job was to bring justice to
wrongdoers, often in imaginative ways: He condemned
Prometheus to have his immortal liver eaten by a huge eagle
forever for the crime of giving fire to humankind, and he
blinded Phineus and sent harpies to torment him for reveal-
ing other godly secrets to humans. He killed Salmoneus
with a thunderbolt for impersonating him and causing fake
storms. He sent Tantalus to be tortured eternally for slaugh-
tering his son and serving him in a feast of the gods.

Temple of Olympian Zeus in Athens.

TEMPLES OF WORSHIP: As the supreme god, Zeus's temples were large and numerous, and they were often the most important in Greek cities. Among the most impressive were the Temple of Olympian Zeus in Athens, which now stands mostly ruined, and the Temple of Zeus at Olympia, also in ruins now. Jupiter, the Roman counterpart of Zeus, was the patron god of Rome, and the people of the city believed that he brought them military victory because they loved him above all others. The temple dedicated to him—along with Juno and Minerva—on Rome's Capitoline Hill was the largest in the region before it was destroyed by fire.

ARTISTIC DEPICTIONS: Zeus is almost always portrayed as a large, bearded man with a scepter and, in Roman times, an eagle. Some archaeologists point out that classical marble statues of Zeus or Jupiter bear a strong resemblance to Renaissance images of the Christian God the Father such as the one on Michelangelo's Sistine Chapel ceiling; but paintings and mosaics of Jupiter show his beard as being black, not white. Relatively few statues of Jupiter have survived intact, partly because when the mad Roman emperor Caligula declared himself a god, he ordered their heads knocked off and replaced with busts of himself.

CHAPTER THREE

Older and Lesser Gods

THE ANNALS OF THE ancients included a host of other gods besides the 12 Olympians. Some were much older, others were newer, still others had narrow spheres of influence in the world or were mainly local in their appeal.

First, there were the "progenitors," gods who existed before the world took on its present form, who separated the light from the darkness, time from space, the sea from the land, and the realm of the living from the land of the dead. These gods did not have corporal forms. They were purely elemental parts of the universe, though that didn't stop human storytellers from using their imaginations and describing the progenitors' physical characteristics for metaphorical purposes. Only a few of them enter mythology directly, but they matter because they define the world's existence itself. You'll find the major ones in this chapter.

Then there were the Titans, a race of giants who ruled the earth during a mythical "Golden Age" before the Olympians came along. Most Olympian gods were descended from the Titans, often in such bizarre ways as virgin birth, rising from chopped-off testicles, or being vomited up by a Titan father who had eaten them. As soon as the first Olympians came on the scene, they went to war against the Titans and took over, apparently a metaphor for the love-hate relationship between teenagers and their parents that continues to this day. Like all gods, the Titans

The forge where Hephaestus made all his creations, including the armor for gods and heroes, was located beneath Sicily's Mount Etna, the largest volcano in Europe.

were immortal, but that didn't stop the Olympians from imprisoning them forever. Some were cast into the pit of Tartarus, a part of the Underworld from which there was no escape, or buried them beneath Mount Etna, the largest volcano in Europe. Others, like Atlas and Prometheus, suffered more creative torments.

Another major category of deities was the Underworld gods. Hades, who presided over them, shared the same ancestry as Zeus and several other Olympians, so you might expect that he would be included among them and have a place at the table on Mount Olympus. But since he almost never left the world of the dead, he presided over a different group of gods. Unlike Hades, some of his underlings came and went from the Underworld in the darkness, bringing dreams, nightmares, and even drug hallucinations to the living mortals on earth.

Other gods, some of them left over from earlier, foreign cultures that had been conquered by the Greeks or Romans, are sometimes referred to as "lesser gods" because their powers are limited and their responsibilities slight. A lesser god might be in charge of sleet and hail, or perhaps gates and doorways, or rainbows, or jealousy. And then there's practically everybody's favorite lesser god, Pan, whose main responsibility seems to be to play his pipes and spread the spirit of spring through the wild places of the earth.

As Greek and Roman mythology evolved, the notion came into vogue that in rare instances gods had the power to turn mortal humans into gods, too. An early instance of this was when Heracles, the mightiest of the Greek demigod heroes, died from centaur-blood poisoning. One version of the legend has it that only the mortal half of him died, while the immortal half became a full-fledged god. Another says that Hera raised him to godhood after his death. In some versions, he was allowed to live among the gods and marry a goddess, whereas in others he was set harmlessly among the constellations of the night sky.

Later, in imperial Rome, some emperors decided that if the gods could bestow immortality, it stood to reason that they could declare themselves gods, too. Whereupon, one may imagine, the deities on Mount Olympus rolled their eyes and declared, "There goes the neighborhood!"

❈ ❈ ❈ ❈

AEOLUS
ROMAN NAME: AEOLUS

Type: Underworld god

Sphere of Influence: Wind

Origins and Myths: Aeolus is a confusing figure in Greek mythology because various tales ascribe the same name to three distinctly different gods with different genealogies and different powers. The one best known today, Aeolus son of Hippotes, was entrusted by Zeus with controlling the storm winds. As winds were often thought of as being horse-shaped, he was also given the title of Hippotades, the "reiner of horses," or he who keeps horses on a tight rein. According to *The Odyssey*, this Aeolus played host to Odysseus and his crew on his floating island, Aeolia. Upon their departure, he gave Odysseus a leather bag full of winds to speed him on his journey home from the Trojan War. But the crew thought the bag was filled with gold and silver, and just before arriving home they greedily opened it while Odysseus was sleeping in an attempt to steal the contents, whereupon the winds escaped all at once, causing a storm that blew their ship back to Aeolia, where the god refused to help them any further. This was one of many misfortunes heaped on Odysseus and his crew as a result of a curse placed on them by the Cyclops Polyphemus. It ulti-

mately took them ten years to sail home to Ithaca, a distance
of only about 650 miles.

❊ ❊ ❊ ❊

ANANKE
ROMAN NAME: NECESSITAS

Type: Progenitor goddess

Sphere of Influence: Inevitability, compulsion,
necessity

Origins and Myths: The daughter of Hydrus (Water)
and Terra (Earth, or Gaea in Greek), Ananke emerged at the
very beginning of time, entwined with her mate Chronos,
the god of time. Together they divided matter, which she
had given birth to as a single giant egg, into its three parts:
heaven, earth, and the sea. They were thus responsible for
creation and the ordering of the universe. As with many of
the progenitor gods, she represented an idea instead of an
element. She had no tangible physical form, though she was
sometimes symbolically depicted in paintings as a winged,
angel-like figure. She was the primal force that causes the
rotation of the heavens, if not movement itself. In some ways
the saying that commemorates her to this day, "Necessity
is the mother of all invention," sums her up best. She is the

"why" and the "what" behind everything we accomplish, the force behind everything that happens. Without her the world and the universe would grind to a halt.

Unlike many of the other progenitor gods and Titans, there is no myth about Ananke being imprisoned after the Olympian gods seized dominion over the earth. Instead, Ananke's legends became intermingled with those of the more recent and much sexier Aphrodite. Eventually, Aphrodite completely replaced Ananke, who played no further role in classical mythology.

❋ ❋ ❋ ❋

ATLAS
ROMAN NAME: ATLAS

Type: Titan

Sphere of Influence: Supporter of the heavens

Origins and Myths: Atlas was one of the second-generation Titan gods. The son of Japetus, his predecessor as God of the West and also god of the mortal life span, and Clymene, goddess of fame, he was said to personify the quality of endurance. He sided with the Titans in their revolt against Zeus and was sentenced to stand on the edge of the earth and support the sky on his back forever. He

turned heaven on its axis, causing the stars to revolve and thus giving men the art of astronomy, helping sailors with navigation and farmers with measuring the seasons so they knew when to plant and harvest their crops. He is most often shown with his head down, shoulders bowed, and one knee on the ground as he stoops under the weight of the world.

While Atlas might have personified endurance, there's probably only so much that one person can take, so when the hero Hercules stopped by and offered him a break from holding up the world for a while, he was only too glad to accept. Perhaps taking further pity on the Titan, Hercules built two great pillars at either end of the earth to help prop it up. Look on a map (or in an atlas) and you'll see that the Pillars of Hercules are the two mountains that flank the Strait of Gibraltar at the west end of the Mediterranean Sea, the farthest extent of the known world in ancient times.

❊ ❊ ❊ ❊

GAEA

ROMAN NAME: TERRA, GAEA, OR TELLUS

Type: Titan

Sphere of Influence: Earth Mother

Origins and Myths: The primordial personification of earth, Gaea first emerged at the dawn of creation, along with air, sea, and sky. She is considered the great mother because so many of the original gods and other creatures—the sea gods, the sky gods, and all mortal beings descend from her. It was also Gaea who convinced Zeus to rise up against Kronos, king of the Titans, and overthrow him. But once Zeus was settled on his throne she became angry with him when he imprisoned her Titan children, Kronos et al., in the pit of Tartarus. She proceeded to produce a race of giants and then the monster Typhone in an attempt to dethrone her grandson. Unfortunately, her king-making abilities had failed her by then, and Zeus and the rest of the Olympian Gods were able to fend off her attempts.

Like the other progenitor gods and goddesses, Gaea never actually had a human form but was imagined as a flat disc surrounded by the great river Okeanos, domed above by the sky, with the pit of hell lying beneath her. Gaea supported the seas and the mountains upon herself. In Greek artwork, however, she was depicted as a large matronly woman half buried beneath the surface of the earth. Later Roman mosaics showed her as a large reclining woman, often clothed in green and accompanied by grain spirits to signify her association with growth and fertility. Of course as Earth Mother she was also associated with everything else natural. She was thought of as uncaring about anything except herself and her offspring; be it tornadoes, floods, hurricanes, or tsunamis, Mother Nature always does what she does, no matter what humans might wish. The Greeks and Romans didn't sentimentalize nature in quite the same way modern humans tend to do.

❈ ❈ ❈ ❈

HADES
ROMAN NAME: PLUTO

TYPE: Underworld god

SPHERE OF INFLUENCE: Lord of the Underworld, including dead mortals and death itself, as well as wealth buried under the earth's surface, such as gold, silver, gemstones, and other precious minerals, as well as the fertile soil that nourishes seeds.

ORIGINS AND MYTHS: Hades was the oldest of three sons of the Titans Kronos and Rhea. After defeating the Titans, the brothers divided control of the world among themselves—the air to Zeus, the sea to Poseidon, and the Underworld to Hades; the three shared dominion over the earth's surface. As King of the Underworld, he was allowed to ascend to the upper realms if he wished, but when he was in his own domain he was completely cut off from the rest of the universe and had no idea what was going on there.

He is generally not considered an Olympian god because he spent so little time on the surface; he was a god of the Underworld, a category unto itself.

Hades kidnapped Persephone, beautiful daughter of Demeter, to be his wife. To settle the rights between father and husband, Zeus decreed that Persephone would spend six months of each year—corresponding to the winter months and early spring—in the Underworld with Hades and the other six months in the upper world. As the god of death, Hades was infertile and unable to father any children.

Hades had no temples or cults dedicated to him in ancient times, though bereaved mortals would offer prayers and sacrifices to him, banging their heads against the ground to get his attention.

❋ ❋ ❋ ❋

HECATE
ROMAN NAME: TRIVIA

Type: Underworld goddess

Sphere of Influence: Crossroads, gates, walls, children, witchcraft, magic, curses, night, moon, ghosts, necromancy

Origins and Myths: The daughter of two Titans, Perses and Asteria, Hecate probably originated as a foreign god.

When her cult spread to Greece she became a source of confusion, since many of her spheres of influence had long since been assigned to other gods, especially Artemis, giving rise to various stories that attempted to explain her presence. In one legend, she arrived as a mortal priestess. Soon after her arrival, she insulted Artemis, who drove her to commit suicide. But in remorse Artemis adorned her corpse with jewelry and resurrected her as a goddess. Among her many other roles, according to this tradition, Artemis appointed her as the avenger of injuries to women.

In other legends, Hecate helped Demeter in her search for her daughter Persephone, who had been abducted by Hades, by guiding her through the night with flaming torches. She went on to become Persephone's minister and companion during her time in the Underworld. While she's usually depicted in drawings and paintings as a young woman carrying three torches, most statues depict her in triple form in her role as goddess of the crossroads. She assisted the Olympians in their war against the giants, so she was one of the few Titans who wasn't imprisoned by Zeus after he overthrew his father.

❈ ❈ ❈ ❈

HESTIA
ROMAN NAME: VESTA

Type: Lesser goddess (Greek), Olympian goddess (Roman)

Sphere of Influence: Hearth, home, family, meals

Origins and Myths: At first this sister of Hades, Poseidon, and Zeus was only worshipped by women inside their homes. As she became more important to the Romans, under the name Vesta, she replaced Bacchus among the Olympian gods. The official explanation was that she had originally been an Olympian in Greece but had stepped down to make room for Dionysus so that the number of gods would not be an unlucky 13. In Rome, Bacchus was removed from the Top 12 when bacchanalias were prohibited, and Vesta was restored so there would be an even balance—six male gods and six female goddesses. A temple was erected for her in the Roman Forum. It was maintained by Vestal Virgins, who kept the sacred flame of the Roman Empire burning. The flame was renewed annually on the date of the Roman new year, March 1, and burned until A.D. 394. Unlike other gods, none of her temples contained any statues representing the goddess.

Hestia was the first child born to Kronos and Rhea and thus became both the first swallowed by her father and the last disgorged when he was forced to spit them out again. In some ways she was both the first and the last of their children to be born, so is both oldest and the youngest. Both Apollo and Poseidon wanted to marry her, but she refused and asked Zeus to let her remain a virgin for all time, a request he honored.

As the goddess of home and hearth, Vesta does not feature in many legends. Her significance lies in the fact as the goddess of the hearth she was also responsible for the fires over which all meals were cooked and is said to have received her own share of every burnt offering of food made to the gods. She is usually depicted as a modestly veiled woman with her right hand resting against her side and her left hand holding a staff or scepter.

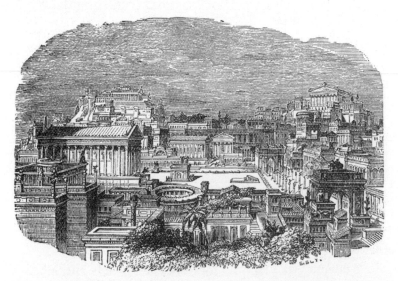

The Roman Forum housed the temple of Vesta. As Vesta became more important to the Romans, she replaced Bacchus (Greek name Dionysus) among the Olympian gods.

HYPERION

ROMAN NAME: HYPERION

Type: Titan

Sphere of Influence: Lord of the East, Lord of Light

Origins and Myths: Hyperion, a son of Uranus and Gaea, was father to all the lights of the heavens, including Helios, the first sun god; Eos, the dawn; and Selene, the first goddess of the moon. He was married to Theia, lady of the *aether*, the shining blue color of the sky. His name literally means either "he who goes above" or simply "watcher from above," both of which relate to his position high in the sky. As both the son of the sky and the father of the sun, moon, and dawn, he was seen as being the god who first ordered the cycles of each and established the regular rhythm of the days and the months. As his name suggests, he had an affinity with observation, and his wife was the goddess of sight. Hyperion and Theia together were believed to have supplied humanity with the gifts of eyes and sight. The Greeks believed the eyes emitted a ray that gave people the ability to see, so the sun and moon, both of which were thought to give off rays, were always associated with sight.

Curiously enough, Hyperion is also the name of the book publishing imprint owned by Disney Book Group that publishes Rick Riordan's Percy Jackson & the Olympians and Heroes of Olympus novels.

✖ ✖ ✖ ✖

HYPNOS
ROMAN NAME: SOPOR

TYPE: Underworld god

SPHERE OF INFLUENCE: Sleep

ORIGINS AND MYTHS: Hypnos was said to reside in a land of eternal darkness, beyond the gates of the rising sun. According to one tale, he lived in a palace that contained no doors or gates so that the creaking of hinges would not wake him up. He planted poppies and other narcotic plants beside the doorway so visitors could join him in his slumber. In another story, he lived in a cave with the River Lethe, bringer of forgetfulness, flowing through it. One of his brothers, Morpheus, was charged with the responsibility of preserving quiet so he could sleep. His other brothers (in Roman tradition they were his sons) Thanatos, god of peaceful death, and Phobetor, god of nightmares, also kept him company in his dark world.

Hypnos rose every night to follow after his mother, Nyx, the Titan goddess of the night, bringing sleep to gods and mortals alike. He is often portrayed as a young man with wings on his brows or shoulders, holding either a horn of opium or a poppy stem, a branch dripping water from the river of forgetfulness, and an inverted torch.

❋ ❋ ❋ ❋

IRIS
ROMAN NAME: ARCUS

Type: Lesser goddess

Sphere of Influence: Rainbows, new endeavors, messenger of the gods, handmaiden to Hera

Origins and Myths: Iris was the daughter of Electra, a cloud nymph and sister to the Harpies, and was fathered by an obscure sea god named Thaumas. She is generally portrayed as a beautiful young woman with golden wings holding a herald's wand in one hand and a water pitcher in the other. After rainstorms, it was she who would gather the water and replenish the clouds. In one version of her legend, her pitcher contained water from the River Styx, which separates the earth from the Underworld; she used it to put perjurers into a deep sleep in order to reveal truth.

Iris was most often referred to as a messenger of the gods. In *The Iliad* she often filled that role, yet in *The Odyssey* she was not mentioned, and Hermes carried messages in her place. Iris traveled as a rainbow, so one of her main attributes was almost instantaneous speed, which made her a suitable consort for her husband, Zephyrus, god of the west wind. Because of the multiple colors of her path through the sky, her name became the source of the word "iridescence."

One of Iris's strangest manifestations was in Euripides's Greek tragedy *Heracles,* where she cursed the future hero with a madness that drove him to murder his wife and children. Heracles was then cursed and assigned to the death-defying labors that would later elevate him to the status of the greatest hero in Greek mythology.

※ ※ ※ ※

JANUS
ROMAN NAME: JANUS APPEARED ONLY IN ROMAN MYTHOLOGY.

Type: Lesser god

Sphere of Influence: Transitions, beginnings and endings, gates and doorways

Origins and Myths: Janus was celebrated at the beginning of the harvest, as well as at planting, marriage, birth, and many other types of new beginnings. He also represented the transitions between primitive life and civilization, rural and urban life, peace and war, and childhood and adulthood. The most famous sanctuary to Janus was in the Roman Forum at the portal through which the legions of

Rome marched when heading off to war. In times of war, the gates to his temple were always left open so he might intervene if required, and then closed again in times of peace. Janus was represented with two faces pointing in opposite directions. In his right hand he held a key, symbolizing his association with the future.

Although most scholars assert that Janus had no counterpart in Greek mythology, quite similar two-faced gods were common in other civilizations including Babylon, Chaldea, Persia, Scandinavia, and parts of India, causing some scholars to theorize that he was imported from one of these cultures, since the Janus Gate in Rome was near a port where foreign ships arrived. Temples believed to have been dedicated to Janus were erected by the Romans in France, Austria, and the Italian cities of Padua and Genoa.

In modern literature, Janus appears as a rather comic figure in *The Battle of the Labyrinth*, the fourth novel of the Percy Jackson & the Olympians saga, as the only Roman character in a story involving the young demigods' encounter with the Greek goddess Hera.

✖ ✖ ✖ ✖

KRONOS
ROMAN NAME: SATURN

TYPE: Titan

SPHERE OF INFLUENCE: Agriculture and the harvest

ORIGINS AND MYTHS: After deposing his father, Kronos became ruler of the cosmos, presiding over a Golden Age with men and animals living in harmony on the Earth and the Earth in turn supplying all of their needs. It is said that men lived like gods and were free from toil, strife, sickness, and cares, never suffered from the debilitating effects of old age, and when they died it was merely as if they fell asleep. Nobody had to work for a living, as fruit and grain grew itself for man's consumption. It was also said that the animals could speak like humans, that there were no states or families, and that Kronos looked after them directly to make sure everybody was well. In fact, the world was supposed to be so ideal that everybody could live outdoors without worrying about clothing or shelter, as Kronos made sure the climate was ideal all the time.

While this sounds pretty picture-perfect, don't forget that Kronos also killed his father, and because of a prophecy that one of this children would kill him in return, every time his wife gave birth he would swallow the child. This went on until she hid one of the children and gave him a rock in swaddling clothes to swallow instead. The child grew up to become Zeus, who freed his siblings and overthrew his father to become ruler of the universe. Instead of committing patricide like his own father did, Zeus merely imprisoned Kronos indefinitely.

Kronos should not be confused with the much older Greek god Chronos, lord of time and old age, who with his consort Ananke separated matter into the sky, the earth, and the sea.

❊ ❊ ❊ ❊

MORPHEUS
ROMAN NAME: SOMNIA

TYPE: Underworld god

SPHERE OF INFLUENCE: Dreams

ORIGINS AND MYTHS: A brother (or son, according to some sources) and attendant of Hypnos, Morpheus was the king of the Oneiroi, the gods or spirits of dreams. In the form of a messenger of the gods, he appeared in prophetic dreams of kings and rulers of men. It is said that he would at times assume the shapes of those who died due to misfortune and appear in the dreams of their closest friends and relatives to inform them of the death. His own shape is unclear, but he was often portrayed as a winged being, which enabled him to fly from place to place. It is said that he could usually be found lying on an ebony bed in a dimly lit cave surrounded by poppies.

"Morpheus" means "he who shapes or molds," and we still use his name today in the context of the word "metamorphosis" to describe someone or something undergoing a change in appearance, as well as in the informal verb "morph." The name of the opiate morphine also has its roots in his name. In the last book of the Percy Jackson & the Olympians series, *The Last Olympian*, Morpheus appears in modern-day New York City to perform a surprising feat.

※ ※ ※ ※

NEMESIS
ROMAN NAME: INVIDIA

TYPE: Lesser goddess

SPHERE OF INFLUENCE: Enmity, fate, rivalry, jealousy

ORIGINS AND MYTHS: Sometimes referred to as Rivalitas, meaning jealous, this goddess's function can be found in the translation of her name: dispenser of dues. Her job was to make sure that everyone got what was coming to them, whether good or bad. She was known as the goddess of retribution for evil deeds and undeserved good fortune. She was also the personification of the resentment people feel toward those who seem to be able to get away with anything or have incredible amounts of good luck. She measured out both happiness and unhappiness, making sure that neither was excessive. If anyone did seem to be getting more than their fair share, she would bring about losses and suffering to redress the balance.

Nemesis is often shown as a winged goddess whose accessories include various instruments of punishment—an apple branch to be used as a switch, a rein to bring someone into check, a lash, a sword, and a set of scales or a balance to measure things out with. In both Rome and Greece, the idea of balance was important, and those who did anything to tip the balance too far in any direction would have to give something back; the gods employed Nemesis to handle that job. The Romans emphasized her role as the goddess of jealous indignation aroused by hubris, the kind of excessive pride that implied placing oneself on the same footing as the gods.

OKEANUS
ROMAN NAME: OCEANUS

Type: Titan

Sphere of Influence: Freshwater rivers and streams

Origins and Myths: Okeanus was the Titan god of the freshwater river the Greeks believed encircled the entire earth, and he was the source of all fresh water, including rainwater, springs, rivers, wells, and lakes. He also regulated the rising and setting of the heavenly bodies that were believed to emerge from and descend into his watery realm at the ends of the earth. His wife, the Titan goddess Tethys, was thought to have distributed her husband's waters around the earth through subterranean caverns. Their children were either river gods or nymphs of springs and fountains.

In Greek art, Okeanus was depicted as a bull-horned god with the tail of a serpentlike fish. Roman art showed him more like a man with crab-claw horns, an oar shaped like a serpent, and a school of fish surrounding him. Tethys, who sat beside him, had wings on her brow signifying her role as the mother of rain clouds. Okeanus and Tethys looked after Hera during the wars between the Titans and the gods, and she came to consider them her foster parents. So great was their affection for Hera that when she asked them to forbid the constellation Ursa Major, the great bear, from setting in their waters they had no trouble agreeing. The constellation had once been a mortal lover of Hera's husband Zeus, and Hera had turned her into a star-bear as punishment.

✳ ✳ ✳ ✳

PAN
ROMAN NAME: FAUNUS, LUPERCUS

TYPE: Lesser god

SPHERE OF INFLUENCE: Wild nature, fertility, springtime

ORIGINS AND MYTHS: Originally a humanlike god, Pan gradually came to be imagined with goatlike features including horns, hooves, and hairy legs. He also assumed the duty of being the protector of herds and flocks, so he was given a second name by the Romans, Lupercus, meaning "he who wards off the wolf." On the Lupercalia (February 15),

priests would march in procession through the streets of Rome wearing goat skins and hitting spectators with goatskin belts.

Roman legend has it that Faunus once challenged Apollo, the god of music, to a contest to see who was the better musician. When they had finished and the judge had awarded Apollo the victory, King Midas—who happened to be in the vicinity and heard both players—declared that he thought the judgment was wrong. Apollo, miffed by the king's unsolicited contradiction, decided that Midas might need bigger ears and so gave him donkey ears. Faunus himself kept a low profile and suffered no punishment.

As the personification of nature, Pan is, of course, unpredictable and wild. It was perhaps this aspect of him that would arouse feelings of panic in men when they would pass near him in wild and remote places. Pan has endured through the ages as a romantic symbol of the wild and uncontrollable aspects of nature. In medieval times, the image of Pan was often equated with Satan. Artists of the Romantic era emphasized the musky sexuality of Pan's nature and often portrayed him with oversized genitals, directing his lust toward nymphs and beasts.

✕ ✕ ✕ ✕

PERSEPHONE
ROMAN NAME: PROSERPINA

Type: Underworld goddess

Sphere of Influence: Queen of the Underworld, after-life, spring growth, and grain

Origins and Myths: The daughter of Demeter and Zeus, Persephone was abducted by Hades with the cooperation of his brother Zeus and forcibly taken to the Underworld to be Hades's wife. It was only when Demeter learned of the role Zeus played in the abduction and threatened the surface with famine unless her daughter was allowed to return to the surface that Persephone was allowed to leave the Underworld. However, as she had eaten some of Pluto's food—a few pomegranate seeds—Persephone was forced to return and spend part of each year in the Underworld. This story explains how the change of seasons came to be, for every year when she returned to her place at her husband's side, the plants would die back and growth would halt, heralding the beginning of winter; when she left the Underworld, the earth celebrated by bringing forth new growth and sending up flowers to mark the start of spring.

Persephone was abducted by Hades and forcibly taken to the Underworld to be his wife.

As her husband was infertile, the only children Persephone bore were the result of her being seduced by other gods, especially her father Jupiter. These offspring included the Furies and Melinoe (another Underworld goddess).

❈ ❈ ❈ ❈

PROMETHEUS
ROMAN NAME: PROMETHEUS

TYPE: Titan

SPHERE OF INFLUENCE: Fire, technology, forethought, crafty counsel

ORIGINS AND MYTHS: Prometheus was entrusted with molding mankind out of clay. He is most famous for trying to help his mortal creations by stealing from the Titan gods. First he stole meat from the sacrificial feasts for them. Then he stole fire to cook it on and so man could both have light in the darkness and warmth in the cold. As punishment for these crimes, he was bound to a stake on Mount Kaukasos, where an eagle (some stories say a vulture) was sent to eat out his liver every day; since he was immortal, the liver would regenerate at night. He was eventually freed by Heracles.

Prometheus was also indirectly responsible for the creation of Pandora, the first mortal woman, and the delivery of misfortune into the house of humans. Zeus wanted to punish mortals because they had received fire from Prometheus. He ordered Pandora's creation from clay and sent her to be the wife of Prometheus's brother, and he gave her a special box that she was never to open. But Pandora's curiosity got the better of her, and when she opened the box she unleashed on the world all the evil and misfortune the gods had stored inside it.

Prometheus has often been cited in modern times as a metaphor for unleashing technology that was beyond man's ability to control. In the 19th century, novelist Mary Shelley subtitled her novel *Frankenstein* "or The Modern Prometheus" because it dealt with bringing an inanimate being to life, and in 2005, with unintended irony, NASA named its effort to launch nuclear reactors into space "Project Prometheus."

❋ ❋ ❋ ❋

RHEA
ROMAN NAME: OPS, CYBELE

TYPE: Titan

SPHERE OF INFLUENCE: "Mother of the gods," female fertility, motherhood, generation, comfort, ease

ORIGINS AND MYTHS: Rhea was the wife of Kronos and the queen of heaven. Although she didn't actually give birth to all the Olympian gods, she did bear many of those considered most important. Literally translated, her name means "flow," referring to a woman's natural cycle of menstruation, birth fluids, and breast milk. Considering all her attributes, there is irony in the trouble she had keeping her own children alive, and the lack of comfort and ease in her marriage. Having to eventually raise a son (Zeus) in secret to prevent her husband from swallowing him alive like he had the rest of their children did not make for a happy marriage. All her children managed to survive being swallowed by their father (no doubt being immortal helped) and seemed none the worse for wear when Kronos was forced to vomit them up later in life. They helped their brother Zeus over-throw Kronos and establish the Olympian pantheon of gods in place of the Titans.

In art, Rhea is shown either sitting on a throne with lions at her sides or riding on a chariot drawn by lions. Unlike most of the Titans, she was not imprisoned after the Olympian overthrow. Though she eventually faded from Greek and Roman mythology, she continued to be worshipped in distant parts of the empire, and when she passed by in her flying chariot, even personages as powerful as Zeus himself and the celebrated hero Jason got out of her path in dread.

❆ ❆ ❆ ❆

URANUS

ROMAN NAME: CAELUS, URANUS

TYPE: Titan

SPHERE OF INFLUENCE: Night sky

ORIGINS AND MYTHS: The god of the sky, Uranus was the husband of Gaea, and fathered the Titans as well as the Cyclopes. The traditional story of Uranus's creation has him as the offspring of Gaea as well. They had many children together, but Uranus hated all of them and hid them away in secret places within Gaea. She set four of her sons—Hyperion, pillar of the East; Crius, pillar of the South; Coeus, pillar of the North; and Japetus, pillar of the West—to pin Uranus in place while Saturn killed him with the sickle made of slate. One of his sons, Kronos, castrated him and threw his genitals into the sea from which Aphrodite was born. His blood that was scattered upon the surface of Gaea turned into both the Furies and the first of the giants. After Uranus's castration, of course, he no longer had relations with Gaea nor sired any more children. His only interaction with the earth from that point forward was to prophecy that Kronos would be overthrown by Zeus and his brothers, setting the stage for the war that brought the Olympian gods to power.

CHAPTER FOUR

Meet the Mythical Beasts and Monsters

THE MONSTERS OF antiquity were the forerunners of the many bizarre creatures that populate comic books and B movies to this day. In Greek and Roman mythology, it can often seem like storytellers invented these horrors and perversities simply to provide heroes like Heracles and Odysseus with worthy adversaries to fight. After all, if it weren't for all the monsters they met along the way, the epic poem of Greek soldiers who spend ten years sailing home from war in a small boat, as recounted in *The Odyssey*, would surely have put audiences to sleep.

But in mythology, monsters represented far more than just hairy, scary evildoers. In antiquity, when the only people who ventured far out of sight of their birthplaces were merchant traders and soldiers, it was easy to imagine any kind of horrific being living just over the horizon in a dank cave strewn with human bones—especially since humans who journeyed into uncharted territory often didn't come back. Stories of monsters and the heroes who fought them mattered because "the devil you know is better than the devil you don't."

On a deeper level, the monsters of Greco-Roman myth represented primal fears. The ancients knew full well that Mother Nature, known among the ancient Greeks and Romans as Gaea, could produce creatures most of us wouldn't think of as "natural." Especially in agricultural societies, many people had witnessed deformities such as a two-headed calf or a child born with a shriveled arm, proof that anything was possible, including things you couldn't even imagine. Then, too, Mediterranean people in Italy, the Middle East, or North Africa may well have seen fossilized skeletons of very large creatures with sharp teeth or footprints with huge claws preserved in sandstone—to them solid evidence that dragons, sea monsters, and giant predators did indeed roam the earth. Thus the world needed heroes to slay them. The 12 labors of Heracles, for instance, were almost all assignments to rid kingdoms of the monsters that had been plaguing their people since time immemorial.

Some of the most famous monsters in Greek and Roman mythology have become icons more familiar to modern

 people than even the gods of Mount Olympus themselves are. Who has not heard of Medusa, the evil woman with the writhing hairdo of poisonous snakes? Or how about the giant Cyclops Polyphemus, a one-eyed giant who hurled boulders from a cliff to sink ships so he could eat the humans aboard? Of course, not all Greek and Roman monsters were bad; some were simply unnatural. Consider the magical race of flying horses known as Pegasus, who were sometimes willing to offer rides to heroes in a hurry, or the Centaurs, half-man and half-horse, some of them wild and warlike but others wise allies of men. Both of these equine beings embodied aspects of the unique relationship between humans and horses that has existed since the earliest times.

In this chapter, we'll meet the most famous monsters and magical creatures in mythology—almost all of whom, by the way, have had close encounters with Percy Jackson.

❃ ❃ ❃ ❃

CENTAUR
ROMAN NAME: CENTAUR

APPEARANCE: Centaurs are made up of the head, shoulders, and torso of a man and the body of a horse.

ORIGIN: In both Greek and Roman legend, there were four distinct tribes of centaurs, each having different origins and behaviors. The Thessalian Centaurs were wild beasts who lived in caves and hunted with sticks and rocks for food. They came into existence as a result of the cloud nymph Nephele being raped by King Ixion of Lapith, and were wiped out when they attended the wedding of Peirithoos, their half brother, and tried to carry off the bride and the female guests. The Peloponnesian Centaurs weren't much different, sharing the same parentage, but are known for their famous battle with Heracles, in which most of them were killed. The Cyprian Centaurs were quite distinct from the others, with bull-like horns growing from their heads. They are said to have been born when Zeus accidently impregnated Gaea after failing to seduce Aphrodite when she first emerged from the sea. The last major group of centaurs, the Lamian Centaurs, started off their lives as river spirits. When Zeus sent them to protect his stepson Dionysus from Hera, she turned them into ox-horned centaurs who served to pull Dionysus's chariot during battle.

Heracles battling a Centaur.

MYTHS AND LEGENDS: Roman stories concerning centaurs are identical to those of the Greeks. Centaurs are gifted fighters and make great cavalry, as they can charge at great speed and fire weapons at the same time. While they have the strength and endurance of a horse plus the intelligence of a man, they are susceptible to wounds from weapons. Like horses, their legs are their most vulnerable spot, and tripping them with ropes or wire makes it easier to defeat them. Chiron, an exceptional Centaur in a number of ways, was accidently wounded by one of Heracles's poisoned arrows. He was in so much pain that he gave up being immortal so he could die. As a reward for his services, instead of sending him to Hades, Zeus gave him a place among the stars as the constellation Sagittarius the Archer, or Centaurus.

WHAT'S NEXT IN HEROES OF OLYMPUS?: The chances of Centaurs showing up on the side of Gaea and the giants in the future are slim. We've already seen examples of how even the wildest of Centaurs have rushed to the rescue of the demigods in Rick Riordan's *The Sea of Monsters* and *The Last Olympian*. One reason they'll stay loyal to the demigods in the future has to do with Chiron, the Centaur who has traditionally been the teacher of heroes since the time of Jason and Achilles. In *The Lightning Thief,* he was the first centaur Percy Jackson met, even if Percy didn't realize it at the time. The legacy of Chiron also lives on in modern depictions of centaurs as wise creatures capable of fortune telling. In her Harry Potter books, J. K. Rowling portrayed them as wild herd animals that were founts of wisdom who fought on the side of good. In his Narnia series, C. S. Lewis showed them as wise and great teachers.

❊ ❊ ❊ ❊

CERBERUS
ROMAN NAME: CERBERUS

Appearance: Cerberus is an enormous three-headed dog, often depicted with the paws of a lion, a mane of serpents, and the tail of a viper; other times he is portrayed as a more or less normal giant hound—except for the three heads, of course.

Origin: Cerberus is said to be the child of the storm giant Typhon and Echidna, the Mother of Monsters. This would make him the brother of the Chimera, the Lernaen Hydra, the Nemean Lion, and the Sphinx.

MYTHS AND LEGENDS: Cerberus guards the entrance to Hades's Underworld, not so much as to keep people from entering but to prevent them from ever leaving once they've stepped into the land of the dead. In Greek mythology, only a few people were ever able to return, and only one of them

managed to sneak past Cerberus. Heracles actually took Cerberus back with him to the land of the living as the last and most dangerous of his 12 great labors. Hades gave Heracles permission to take the giant dog as long as he could subdue him without using weapons, whereup-

Cerberus with Heracles.

on Heracles did so and took Cerberus back to Eurystheus, the king who had assigned him the labor. Ironically, when he saw the dog face-to-face, Eurystheus was so terrified that he begged Heracles to return it to the Underworld and, in exchange, ruled that Heracles would not have to perform any more labors. Orpheus, in his abortive attempt to rescue his wife from Hades, was able to lull the dog to sleep with a song on his lyre. The Roman hero Aeneas and the goddess Psyche were able to sneak past Cerberus by appealing to his sweet tooth and feeding him honey cakes.

In *The Lightning Thief*, Annabeth discovers that Cerberus is just a big puppy at heart, but if you don't have experience with dog obedience classes you might not want to risk trying to get him to heel. A modern version of Cerberus makes an appearance in J. K. Rowling's book *Harry Potter and the Philosopher's Stone (Sorcerer's Stone)* in the shape of Fluffy, a three-headed dog helping to protect the Philosopher's Stone from Lord Voldemort. Just like Orpheus, Harry is able to lull Fluffy to sleep with flute music.

What's Next in Heroes of Olympus?: For all his viciousness, Cerberus is not really an enemy to demigods. In fact, he's in the employ of the Olympians and very loyal to his master, Hades (Pluto), and he seems to have struck up a friendship with the ultimate demigod, Heracles. The chances of him joining a giant revolution and trying to overthrow the gods are slim, and unless one of our heroes finds him or herself consigned to the Underworld, they shouldn't come into conflict with him.

CHIMERA
ROMAN NAME: CHIMAERA

Appearance: The Chimera had the head and body of a lion, a goat's head rising from its back, and the head of a serpent on its tail.

Origin: This is a particularly nasty creature, as you'd pretty well expect of a child of Typhon and Echidna. There are also references to Chimera-type creatures predating both the Greeks and the Romans. The Hittite chimera, which probably served as the basis for the myth, was a creature with a main human head, a lion's head facing forward, and a snake's head on the end of its tail. A version of the Chimera also showed up in the art of the Etruscans, the kingdom that ruled the Italian peninsula before the Romans.

Myths and Legends: If you ever find yourself in Lycia, Turkey, look for a series of vents in a hill overlooking what used to be a temple to Hephaestus that emit flaming methane gas and are thought to have given birth to the story of the fire-breathing Chimera living in the surrounding hills. If you should find yourself facing a Chimera, be especially wary of its ability to breathe fire and the fact that it can see in more than one direction at once. Sneaking up on it will be extremely difficult, but its goat head is less dangerous than its fire-breathing lion head or the poisonous fangs of its serpent-headed tail, so you might want to tackle it from the side if possible. Like all other monsters, it is suscepti-ble to attacks by Celestial Bronze weapons. Try a bow and arrow or a javelin. If you move quickly enough and follow up your throw with a direct attack, the javelin might distract it enough for you to get in a swing with a sword before the Chimera recovers enough to strike. The original Chimera had two children, the Sphinx and the Nemeian Lion, and was slain by the hero Bellerophon riding on Pegasus, the original winged horse.

WHAT'S NEXT IN HEROES OF OLYMPUS?: Percy Jackson barely escapes with his life when he faces the Chimera on his first quest as a demigod in *The Lightning Thief*. As the child of the storm giant Typhon, the Chimera might hold a grudge against the Olympians for taking down his father—again—along with the fact that the only reason Zeus lets his mother live is to breed monsters who could serve as chal-lenges to future heroes. We may not have seen the last of the Chimera yet.

※ ※ ※ ※

CYCLOPES
ROMAN NAME: CYCLOPES
(SINGULAR = CYCLOPS)

Appearance: While the stories about the Cyclopes changed over the years, their basic characteristics as giant, one-eyed creatures skilled in metal work remain consistent throughout their mythology.

Origin: The three original Cyclopes were the sons of Uranus and Gaea and were named Arges, Steropes, and Brontes. Uranus threw them into Tartarus, the pit of hell, from which they were rescued by Kronos when he overthrew his father. However, he immediately returned them to the pit once he succeeded in his revolt, and they remained there until freed by Zeus when he overthrew his father, Kronos. In gratitude for being freed, the three made Zeus's lightning bolt, Hades's battle helmet, and Poseidon's trident.

Myths and Legends: The Cyclopes legend started to get confused when Homer described them as man-eating giants who lived in the southwestern part of Sicily. Then they became a race of shepherds who lived in caves. Chief among them was the beast Polyphemus, whom Odysseus fooled by making himself invisible and calling himself "Nobody." Having only one eye doesn't seem to hinder the Cyclopes' ability to see, though it probably affects their depth perception. In the case of Polyphemus, Odysseus was able to blind him by stabbing him in the eye. The meaner the Cyclops, it seems, the lower its intelligence, and a hero who keeps his wits about him stands a good chance of escape. An even later tradition has the Cyclopes reverting back to being useful members of the Olympian society and becoming assistants of the god Hephaestus, making the metal armor and ornaments for the gods. Although their numbers increased to more than the original three in this later inter-pretation, it is consistent with the earliest description of the

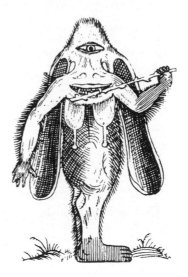

three brothers being skilled metal workers. In his epic Latin poem *The Aeneid,* Virgil describes an island off the coast of Sicily called Volcania where the Cyclopes worked at forges building the various objects for the gods and describes them as continually making thunderbolts for Jupiter (Zeus).

Percy, Annabeth, and Tyson (himself a demi-Cyclops) have to deal with Polyphemus during their quest recounted in *The Sea of Monsters,* and he is just as unpleasant with them as he had been with Odysseus. More famous yet is the modern Cyclops, a Marvel Comics superhero who is a member of the X-Men; he can shoot a beam of concentrated light from his eyes and has to wear a visor at all times to control his power.

WHAT'S NEXT IN HEROES OF OLYMPUS?: While some Cyclopes are on the side of the Olympians, they are also the children of Gaea, and the evil-tempered ones like Polyphemus have longstanding grudges against heroes and demigods. If given the opportunity, they'd be more than willing to join the rebellion and do their best to kill as many of their old foes as possible.

❈ ❈ ❈ ❈

DRAKONES
ROMAN NAME: DRACONES

APPEARANCE: "Drakon" was the generic term used by the Greeks to describe any dragon-type creature, ranging from giant snakes and sea monsters to the winged dragons found throughout folklore.

ORIGIN: Among the many drakon species known to the Greeks were the Aithiopkoi or Ethiopian Drakon—described as gigantic serpents over 180 feet long, some of the longest-lived creatures around that were not truly immortal, and capable of eating elephants—and the Lydian Drakon, the largest drakon ever known, over 200 feet in length and as wide as a school bus, capable of spitting poisonous venom and paralyzing warriors by mere eye contact. Neither of these species had wings, but the Medean Sun Drakones did. They were so named because they once belonged to the first god of the sun, Helios, and pulled his chariot across the sky. He gave them to his granddaughter Medea, for whom they performed the same service. The Sun Dragons had golden wings and bright orange eyes that had the same paralyzing power as their larger cousins'. While the Romans called the species by a similar name, some of the individual names were quite different. In Roman myths, Dracones Rapuere were the pair that pulled Medea's chariot.

Myths and legends: Most demigods and heroes worth their salt have crossed paths with a drakon at one time or another. If you run into one, you know you're in for a fight: If the sheer size of the thing doesn't overwhelm you, a drakon can paralyze you if it makes eye contact, it can spit venom and/or breathe fire, its claws can tear you apart, and its tail can knock you silly. It also has teeth that can shred steel and wings that give it an advantage in maneuvering. Often, a drakon's only vulnerabilities are its eyes. Once it's blinded, you can finish it off with a spear or javelin.

Percy Jackson and the rest of the demigods at Camp Half-Blood won't soon forget their encounter with the

Lydian Drakon in *The Last Olympian,* or Tyson's close encounters with the Aethiopian (in *The Sea of Monsters* and *The Battle of the Labyrinth*) and Scythian (*The Sea of Monsters*) breeds. Greek Drakones were, of course, only one example of the mythological beasts known around the world, from the Middle East to China to the Mesoamerican land of the Maya. And what fan can forget Harry Potter's duel with the dragon in J. K. Rowling's *Harry Potter and the Goblet of Fire*, one of several appearances by the flying fire-breathers in that series?

WHAT'S ΠEXT IΠ HEROES OF OLYΠPUS?: While Gaea is sure to rely on her giant children to do most of the fighting in any future conflict, she'd be silly not to try to enlist the help of some of these powerful creatures. Jason, Leo, and Piper have already had a showdown with the Medean Drakones, which they only manage to survive with the help of their automaton in *The Lost Hero*. It's a good bet that this is just the warm-up act and there will be more to follow.

※ ※ ※ ※

ECHIDNA
ROMAN NAME: ECHIDNA

Appearance: Echidna is described as having the head and torso of a beautiful woman and the slimy body of a sea serpent.

Origin: Echidna was the daughter of Gaea and the Titan Tartarus, according to many legends. Others say she was born of two ancient sea gods, Ceto and Phorcys, or of the Chrysaor, a winged boar who was Pegasus's brother. In some versions of her legend, she lives in the pit of Tartarus, where many early monsters were confined by the Olympians. Although monsters confined to Tartarus generally aren't happy and try to escape at every opportunity, many descriptions of Echidna suggest that she is quite pleased to make her home there. Other legends have her living in a cave at Arima, a mysterious place "far from the immortal gods, and far from all mortals," according to the Greek poet Hesiod.

Myths and Legends: Consort of the storm giant Typhon, Echidna is best known as the mother of some of the foulest monsters ever to terrorize the Mediterranean region, including the multiheaded dogs Orthos and Cerberus; the especially nasty nine-headed Hydra, the abominations known as Khimaira and Sphinx; Scylla, Medusa, and her Gorgon sisters; various drakones; and perhaps the Nemean Lion. After the first Titan Wars, when Zeus overthrew Kronos, he decided not to consign Echidna to the pit of Tartarus so she and her children could provide challenges for future heroes (who no doubt were grateful for his thoughtfulness.) While she may not have possessed the array of weapons other monsters did, Echidna was considered extremely powerful because of her immortality and because she had been around since near the beginning of time. She was older than some of the gods themselves, and her mere presence was enough to overcome all but the bravest of heroes. Often accompanied by one her monstrous brood, she had no real weaknesses and was a formidable adversary for even the greatest of heroes. Although her name translates as either "poisonous snake" or "viper," nowhere in mythology is she described as actually being poisonous.

Percy Jackson met Echidna and one of her offspring, a Chimera, while on his first quest in *The Lightning Thief* and has run into a few of her other monster-children since. Two of the more exotic are Dracanina Delphyne (Serpent Womb, a reference to the number of snakelike monsters she gave birth to) and Myraina Tartesia (the Eel of Tartarus).

WHAT'S NEXT IN HEROES OF OLYMPUS?: As the wife of the storm giant Typhon, Echidna is likely to hold a grudge against both the Olympian gods and demigods of all shapes and sizes. If her mother, Gaea, asks for help, there's not much chance Echidna or her children refuse.

❇ ❇ ❇ ❇

GORGONS
ROMAN NAME: GORGONS

APPEARAΠCE: The Gorgon sisters were winged, covered with impenetrable scales, and had sharp fangs, beards, and hands made of brass. Medusa's hair was a writhing mass of snakes, and her gaze could turn men to stone.

ORiGiΠ: The Gorgons were the daughters of Phorcys, the ancient god of the seas, and Keto, goddess of deep-sea creatures, ancient beings that lived long before the Titans. The three sisters—Stheno, Euryale, and Medusa—were among the oldest monsters in European mythology; depictions of them have been found on pottery, clay masks, and cave paintings dating back to around 4000 B.C., long before the rise of the Greek civilization. Of the three, only Medusa was mortal. According to later Greek legends, Medusa was originally a beautiful maiden, but the goddess Athena turned her into a snake-haired monster as punishment for making love to Poseidon in a temple to Athena.

Myths and Legends: The Gorgons, especially Medusa, have figured in numerous legends over the centuries. The most famous is that of Perseus, the first of the great Greek demigod heroes, who was sent on a quest to bring the head of Medusa back to the king. Armed with borrowed weapons—Zeus's sword, Athena's shield, Hades's helm of darkness, and Hermes's flying sandals—Perseus went to the cave where the Gorgon sisters were sleeping and cut off Medusa's head, escaping the others with the help of Hades's helm. From Medusa's neck sprang the flying horse

Pegasus, and drops of her blood turned into poisonous snakes. Perseus kept the severed head, which retained the power to turn to stone anyone who looked at its face, and used it as a weapon in other battles. He turned the Titan Atlas to stone, forming the Atlas Mountains of Morocco, and saved his mother from a forced marriage by petrifying her would-be husband. Finally he gave the head to the goddess Athena, who decorated her shield with it. Throughout Greece, busts of Medusa were placed on Athena's temples to protect them.

WHAT'S ΠEXT iΠ HEROES OF OLYΜPUS?: As Perseus proved by killing many of his enemies with Medusa's head after he cut it off, Medusa is a threat even in death. Being immortal, she has the ability to come back to life after a time and cause further trouble. In *The Lightning Thief,* Percy, Annabeth, and Grover face Medusa early in their first quest, and later in the same book Percy's mother uses the Medusa head to rid herself of her husband, Gabe. Who knows whose hands it could turn up in next? Medusa was never fond of the Olympians—or of humans in general—so if Gaea were to invite her to join a new rebellion, you can bet she'd be right in there. Perhaps her sister Gorgons, who harbor a grudge against Percy Jackson for slaying Medusa, would join her.

※ ※ ※ ※

HARPIES
ROMAN NAME: HARPYIA

APPEARANCE: Depicted as winged women with wizened and ugly faces, the Harpies are sometimes said to have the lower bodies of birds. More fanciful descriptions say they have the heads of roosters on the bodies of women, with huge claws and faces worn out from their insatiable hunger.

ORIGIN: The Harpies were offspring of sea god Thaumus and his consort, Electra. Their Roman name, "Harpyia," literally translates as "snatchers." These spirits of sudden gusts of wind, also known as the Hounds of Zeus, were dispatched by Zeus to snatch people and things from earth. Individual Harpy names reflected their windy heritage: Aello means "storm wind" or "whirlwind"; Aellopos (Roman name Aellopus) means "storm-footed"; and Podarke (Roman name Podarce) means "fleet-footed."

MYTHS AND LEGENDS: A Thracian king, Phineas, had the ability to see the future. Zeus became angry at him for telling too much, so he exiled Phineas to an island where the Harpies would appear and steal all his food before he could eat it. Jason arrived with his Argonauts, drove the Harpies away, and got Zeus to agree that they would not return. In another myth, one of the Harpies' duties was to torment people on their way to the pits of hell. Depending on whose

version of the Harpies a hero winds up facing—Roman
or Greek—the danger they pose could vary from being
snatched suddenly from the earth's surface and carried
away to some place designated by Zeus, to being torn apart
by fearsome claws and then eaten by the creatures. Either
way, the Harpies' main weapons appear to be their speed
and their ability to dart in and out of places quickly, combined with fearsome claws and fangs. Any weakness they
might have would be hard to exploit because of their speed,
and if they take you by surprise, they could easily carry you
away before you even know it. As with any winged monster,
your best chance for defeating them lies in a bow or another
type of long-range weapon. Actually, your best bet is making

sure you don't do anything to attract their attention in the first place. Avoiding Zeus's anger is always a good plan, anyway.

Percy Jackson runs into the Harpies in *The Sea of Monsters.* While you won't find many Harpies flying around these days, we still use the word "harpy" to refer to a mean older woman. When you call someone an "old harpy," everyone knows you mean she isn't very nice and should be avoided. For some reason, many unpopular math teachers seem to be harpies.

What's Next in Heroes of Olympus?: As these creatures are the servants of Zeus, the chances of them allying themselves with Gaea in a forthcoming war are slim. However, they are wind spirits, and we've already seen how they are used against demigods in *The Lost Hero.*

❋❋❋❋

LERNAEAN HYDRA

ROMAN NAME: LERNAEAN HYDRA

Appearance: The Hydra was a nine-headed serpent that lived in a cave by the swamps of Lake Lerna. As if all those heads weren't bad enough, each time you managed to cut one off, two more would grow back in place of the original. The creature's bile was venomous, so if you were bitten by it, there was a good chance you would die of your wounds. The Romans seemed to delight in embellishing the worst characteristics of the monsters they inherited from the Greeks, and the Hydra was no exception. Not being satisfied with its bite being poisoned, the Romans made it so vile that not only would its breath alone kill you, but if you walked near it while it was asleep and inhaled, you would die some time later in great torment.

Origin: The Hydra was a child of the titan Typhon and Echidna, the Mother of Monsters. Hera raised it for the sole purpose of killing Heracles.

Myths and Legends: Conquering the Hydra was Heracles's second labor, which he accomplished by enlisting the help of his nephew, who cauterized each of the monster's necks with a torch as soon as Heracles chopped the head off, preventing it from growing back. Heracles later used blood from the Hydra to poison arrows for fighting other monsters.

To get an idea of just how difficult a task it is to face off against the Hydra, you only have to look at what it took for Percy, Annabeth, Tyson, and Clarisse to defeat it in *The Sea of Monsters*. Even with the power of a Cyclops to help them, Percy and Annabeth required backup from the cannons on Clarisse's ship. While there have been many examples of multiheaded villains in mythology, one of the more

novel examples of the Hydra in contemporary storytelling came from Marvel Comics, which created a league of super-villains called themselves The Hydra. The Hydra prided themselves on being so completely secret that no one ever knew the identities of their members, and their numbers were so great that if a superhero managed to take one member out of business, two more would be right there to take the vanquished one's place.

WHAT'S ⎺EXT i⎺ HEROES OF OLYⅢPUS?: Being one of the children of Typhon makes the Hydra a grandchild of Gaea, which means there is a good chance she'll be seen in the future. Gaea is unlikely to pass up the opportunity to make use of any family members at her disposal, especially one as nasty as this.

MANTICORE
ROMAN NAME: MANTICHORA

Appearance: The Manticore was a fabulous man-eating monster with the body of a lion and the face of a man with a snake-tipped, arrow-shooting tail. It had triple rows of teeth, the ears of a human, and a voice that sounded like a panpipe blended with a trumpet, as well as the ability to mimic human speech. It measured around ten feet in length and was bloodred in color.

Origin: The name Manticore was derived from a Persian word meaning "man-eater." Even the Greeks gave the animal's origins as Indian or Middle Eastern, and the myth itself came from Persia (modern day Iran).

Myths and Legends: The Manticore has a fearsome variety of weapons at its disposal from front to back. It can savage you at close range with tooth and claw or sit back and shoot poison darts at you from its tail. The stings might not kill you, but like any scorpion sting they will slowly

freeze your limbs and make you an easy target for the rest
of the creature's weapons. Thankfully, the Manticore is not
armored, so if you can fend off its attacks, you have a good
chance of inflicting damage. Your best bet for dealing with
a Manticore is to make sure you can employ some sort of
shield or work in tandem with a demigod. If you can keep
your shield up as a defense against the darts, you may be
able to work close enough to stab it with a celestial bronze
weapon. Percy Jackson and his friends run into the Manticore on more than one occasion when dealing with Atlas.
Annabeth, Thalia, Grover, and Percy have to deal with the
Manticore in *The Titan's Curse* and ended up in the fight of
their lives against it, surviving only by the timely interven-
tion of the goddess Artemis and her huntresses.

What's Next in Heroes of Olympus?: While there's no doubt the Manticore is a formidable enemy and would be of use to Gaea against the demigods in the upcoming giant war, he's not one of her children. He's not even Greek. While he has fought for the Titans in the past, he also acts as a bit of a free agent; in *The Titan's Curse,* he takes on Percy Jackson and his friends on without any backup and, at one point, against orders in an attempt to prove his worth to Atlas. Gaea probably doesn't think too highly of this and would more likely count on her family and those she's most familiar with to make up her army.

MEDUSA

(See GORGONS)

MINOTAUR

ROMAN NAME: MINOTAUR

Appearance: The head of a bull on the giant torso of a man made the Minotaur fearsome enough, but his appetite for human flesh marked him as a creature you'd really want nothing to do with. The Minotaur is immensely strong and armed with fearsome horns, with which he will attempt to gore a man or demigod. He's also very fast.

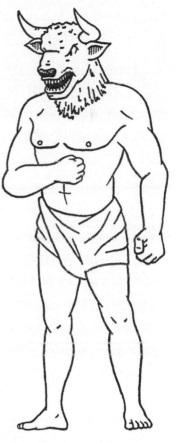

ORIGIN: The Minotaur was born as a result of Pasiphae, the wife of King Minos of Crete, mating with an immense bull that Poseidon had sent Minos as a gift to be used as a sacrifice. Before Minos and the creature named for him, bulls were sacred on the island of Crete. In elaborate bull dances, men and women would propel themselves over bulls by grabbing hold of their horns and flipping themselves onto and over the creatures' backs. When Minos decided to keep the huge bull instead of sacrificing it, the god of the sea infected his wife with a madness that made her want to mate with the bull. She had Minos's court inventor, Daedalus, build her the frame of a cow, which she used to trick the bull into mating with her.

MYTHS AND LEGENDS: When the Minotaur was born, Minos ordered Daedalus to build the famous labyrinth as a prison for him. Anyone who then displeased him or whom he wished to sacrifice would be sent into the labyrinth and be killed and eaten by the Minotaur. In the end, the Greek hero Theseus was able to kill the monster, but only with the aid of Minos's daughter Ariadne. She had fallen in love with the young hero and provided him with a ball of magical string that he could use to find his way back out of the labyrinth. The Romans told much the same story about this creature in their legends and didn't even change the spelling of his name.

Thankfully, not only does the Minotaur have the head of a bull, he also seems to have the brain of one, too, which means he quickly becomes blind with rage. His other weakness is a lack of maneuverability. He might be fast in a straight line, but he doesn't turn easily, and like an out-of-control freight train, he can't exactly stop on a dime. He can be defeated if you goad him into a blind rage so he's not thinking straight, then position yourself in front of something hard and strong, like a mountain; when he charges, leap out of the way at the last minute. The crash might not kill him, but it will stun him enough for you to move in and finish him off.

The Minotaur is both one of the first monsters Percy Jackson faces in *The Lightning Thief* and one he takes on in combat alone in the last battle of the Titan War in *The Last Olympian*.

WHAT'S NEXT IN HEROES OF OLYMPUS?: Gaea seems to have no trouble reviving any of the giant monsters and recruiting them to her cause, so chances are the Minotaur will be poking his horned head into the fray again. He's not too fond of Greeks, except as snacks, so he'd probably leap at the chance to take them on again.

※ ※ ※ ※

NEMEAN LION
ROMAN NAME: LEO NEMAEUM

APPEARANCE: This extralarge male lion was made even more dangerous by his hide, which was impervious to all weapons.

ORIGIN: The parentage of this monster is debatable. Some say he resulted from a union between the two-headed dog Orthros and the Chimera. Others assert that he was a child of the Titan Typhon, and in some Roman tales he was a piece of the moon goddess Selene that fell to earth after she nursed him until he was weaned and able to fend for himself.

MYTHS AND LEGENDS: This monster lived in a cave near Archaia Nemea, an ancient Greek town that is now a popular archaeological site. The lion would kidnap young women and hold them hostage until a hero arrived to rescue them. It would lie in the gloom of the cave, pretending to be injured, until the hero would come near enough for the lion to devour it. It was considered such a threat that the first labor demanded of Heracles was to destroy it. The hero used his great strength to strangle the beast, then skinned it to make the lion-skin cape he would wear throughout his career. A hero would find fighting a giant lion to be bad enough, as he'd have to confront its teeth and claws, but one whose skin repulses all weapons? He might strike at the eyes of the Nemean Lion as a possible point of vulnerability, trying to shoot an arrow through one of them into its brain. But that's an awfully small target to be aiming at when such a fearsome beast is charging at you. Heracles probably had the best idea, choking the life out of it, though it's hard to imagine that an adolescent demigod would have the strength to do that. In *The Titan's Curse,* Percy Jackson is luckily able to use samples of freeze-dried astronaut food to gag the beast.

While demigods are often in conflict with the Nemean Lion, the same isn't necessarily true for all Olympians. Hera is said to have hated Heracles so much—he was her husband's son by another woman, after all—that she either helped many of the monsters he faced or went out of her way to honor them after he defeated them. This was the case with the Nemean Lion, and after Heracles killed it, Hera created the constellation Leo to commemorate it.

WHAT'S NEXT IN HEROES OF OLYMPUS?: If, like other cats, the Nemean Lion has nine lives, he might show up again to pit claw and fang against the demigods. He's big and tough, so it's even money Gaea will give him another chance to take a bite out of a demigod or two.

❋ ❋ ❋ ❋

PEGASUS
ROMAN NAME: PEGASUS

APPEARANCE: Pegasus is depicted as a horse, usually white in color, with long, broad, birdlike wings capable of supporting not only his formidable weight but that of an adult human rider. Not only are Pegasus and his descendants capable of flying for great distances but they are also capable war horses. With their ability to swoop down upon an enemy swiftly enough to avoid most weapons tossed their way, they serve as a means of conducting both aerial combat and scouting. They also pack a mean wallop when they kick, but their primary asset is their ability to fly, and their greatest weakness is that since they aren't armored, no matter how fast they are, they can be shot in the back with an arrow.

ORIGIN: Pegasus, whose name means "spring forth," sprang out of the severed neck of Medusa (*see* Gorgons) when she was slain by Perseus. Because of the tale that says Athena turned Medusa from a lovely maiden into a snake-haired monster after catching her making love to the sea god in one of her temples, Roman sources say that Poseidon was Pegasus's father. However, earlier versions of the story don't mention this significant detail and simply have the mighty horse appearing magically when Medusa is decapitated.

MYTHS AND LEGENDS: Pegasus, the immortal winged horse, was the father of all winged horses. He now appears as the constellation named after him in the Northern Hemisphere night sky. The first sight of his constellation every

year marks the arrival of spring and warmer weather, which gives his name a double meaning, as spring is a period of rebirth when new life blossoms forth from the earth. There is also a legend that in ancient times, wherever Pegasus stamped the earth with his foot, a pure mountain spring would burst forth.

Two of the most famous winged horses to survive from the ancient world are a pair of terra-cotta sculptures that were found in a tomb from the Etruscan era in the city of Tarquinia, formerly known as Civita. The two horses appear to have once been attached to a chariot of an unknown god of the Etruscans. In the great classical Indian epic story the *Mahabharata*, the great warrior of God named Kalki is said to have ridden a white horse who was as fast on land as he was in the sky. According to Islamic belief, the prophet Mohammed was supposed to have ascended to heaven upon the back of a white winged horse named Burak.

WHAT'S ɄEXT iɄ HEROES OF OLYɄPUS?: Pegasus isn't the kind of monster that any of the heroes of Olympus are ever going to have to fight. In fact, the children of Pegasus have been faithful and loyal companions to demigods. Like all young demigods at Camp Half-Blood, Percy Jackson receives basic instruction on how to fly a Pegasus in *The Sea of Monsters*. He also became especially bonded with one in particular, Blackjack in *The Sea of Monsters* and *The Titan's Curse*.

SCYLLA & CHARYBDIS

ROMAN NAMES: SCYLLA & CHARYBDIS

Appearance: Charybdis, an immortal being who gulps down everything she can swallow, appears to mortals as a whirlpool beside the rock she lives on, which forms one side of the Straits of Messina, separating the boot heel of Italy and the island of Sicily. Directly opposite her stand the enormous cliffs where Scylla lives. A fearsome creature, Scylla has 12 dangling feet and six long necks. A triple row of fangs lines each of her heads.

Origin: Charybdis was a daughter of the god Poseidon and Gaea, the personification of the earth. Charybdis has been described as a woman with a huge appetite who one day stole oxen from Heracles. As punishment for her theft, Zeus hurled her into the sea with his thunderbolt. So now, instead of swallowing enormous amounts of food, she swallows the sea and spits it back up three times a day. As for Scylla, most stories refer to her father as Phorkys, an ancient sea god who ruled giant creatures living in the depths, and her mother as his wife Keto, whose name literally means "sea monster."

MYTHS AND LEGENDS: In Homer's *Odyssey* and other tales, sailors attempting to pass through the Straits of Messina would try to avoid being sucked to the bottom of the ocean by Charybdis only to have Scylla's six long necks swoop down on them and grab a sailor in each mouth. The saying "between Scylla and Charybdis" means the same as "between a rock and a hard place." If you ever need to pass through the Straits of Messina, you're going to have your hands full trying to deal with these two. If you don't get caught and sucked down to the bottom of the sea by Charybdis when she inhales or run aground and then submerged when she exhales, Scylla will swoop down from her clifftop and scoop up your crew in her fearsome maws. Unfortunately, neither seems to have any real weaknesses or

Charybdis is an immortal being who gulps down everything she can swallow.

Scylla, also known as Phorkys, is an ancient sea god who ruled giant creatures living in the depths.

vulnerabilities, especially when they work in tandem. Odysseus managed to pass through the straits on a raft by grabbing hold of the branches of a fig tree growing on Charybdis's island as she sucked the water in. When she spat it out again and the raft resurfaced, he reclaimed it and paddled away as quickly as he could.

Percy Jackson and his companions have to pass through the Straits of Messina on their quest to find the Golden Fleece and rescue their friend in *The Sea of Monsters*. They barely escape with their lives, and their ship is destroyed.

What's Next in Heroes of Olympus?: Fortunately, the chances of either one of these two posing any threats to Rick Riordan's heroes in the future is minimal. Since their locations are fixed, they're not likely to be involved in any conflict between the giants and the Olympians. The young demigods are unlikely to return to the Sea of Monsters, though in the complex world of mythology, anything is possible.

�֍ ✖ ✖ ✖

SEIRENES
ROMAN NAME: SIRENS

Appearance: Most commonly referred to by their Roman nmes, the Sirens are described either as having only the heads of women attached to the bodies of birds or as women with the legs and wings of birds. Their weapon is their voices; if you hear them you will be immediately ensnared and won't be able to prevent yourself from attempting to reach them.

Origin: These three sea nymphs were once handmaidens to the goddess Persephone. After Persephone was abducted by Hades, her mother, Demeter, gave the three nymphs the bodies of birds so they could aid in the search for the missing goddess. They eventually gave up the search and settled on an island. According to most tales, their father was the god Akheloios—the spirit of the Aitolia River, the largest freshwater river in Greece—and their mother was one of the muses, although there is no agreement as to which one. There is even more confusion surrounding the names of the individual Sirens, as no one seems to agree on what they were called. At least one was called some variation of the Greek word for charming, *thelxis*, but whether it was Thelxiope (charming voice), Thelxinoe (charming the mind), or Thelxiepeia (charming) is unclear. A second was called either Aglaophonos (splendid sounding) or Aglaope (splendid voice), while the third could have been any of the following: Molpe (song), Peisinoe (affecting the mind), Parthenope (maiden voice), or Ligeia (clear-toned).

MYTHS AND LEGENDS: The Sirens lured passing sailors to their deaths by singing so seductively the sailors would lose their senses and wreck their ships on the rocks surrounding the island. They appear in any number of stories in both Greek and Roman mythology. It is said that after they suffered defeat at the hands of Heracles, the wild centaurs fled from him by water, only to be ensnared by the song of the Sirens and starve to death. On another occasion, the goddess Hera encouraged the Sirens to challenge the Muses to a singing competition. When they lost, the Muses plucked out the Sirens' feathers and made crowns for themselves. A statue of Hera in one of her sanctuaries shows her carrying the three Sirens in her hands following their defeat. Most famous of all were their appearances in both the tale of Jason and his Argonauts and Homer's account of the travels of Odysseus. The Argonauts managed to safely navigate past their island only because Orpheus drowned out their voices with a song of his own, while Odysseus had himself tied to the mast of his boat to keep him from giving into the temptation of their song. He also took the precaution of having all his sailors plug their ears with wax to prevent them from being affected. In modern usage, a "siren" means something that sounds a warning of danger, whether it's on a fire engine or signaling an air raid. We also use the phrase "siren's call" to describe any sound that is both seductive and dangerous.

Percy Jackson and Annabeth have a run-in with the Sirens in *The Sea of Monsters* and only barely escape.

WHAT'S NEXT IN HEROES OF OLYMPUS?: As it seems likely the heroes may have to make a voyage to Greece, as hinted at in *The Lost Hero,* they may have to sail past the island of the Sirens to get there. Even if Leo succeeds in building a flying boat, that won't guarantee safe passage past their voices.

CHAPTER FIVE

MORE MONSTERS

SOME MYTHOLOGICAL monsters were immortal, while others could be killed. This usually had to do with whether an immortal god played a role in creating them. Many of the monsters Heracles fought in his 12 labors vanished from mythology after he slew them. Other monsters, however—even if they were burned completely or disintegrated into dust—could pull themselves together and rise up to terrorize the populace once more, even though it might take centuries for them to reappear.

Consider the strange case of Medusa, the serpent-coifed Gorgon woman who could turn people to stone with her gaze. She was killed by Perseus, the first of the great Greek heroes, after whom Percy Jackson was named. Perseus chopped off her head and gave it as an offering to the goddess Athena, who set it on her shield as a coat of arms. Yet that didn't stop her from appearing in later Roman epics such as Ovid's *Metamorphosis,* or, in modern times, being immortalized in bronze by surrealist artist Salvador Dali in the middle of a pedestrian plaza in Marbella, Spain. Nor does it stop her from trying to turn Percy Jackson and his pals to stone in *The Lightning Thief.*

One thing is for certain about the monsters of ancient Greece and Rome: There sure were a lot of them, each one different. Perhaps the most common variety was those that were made up of parts of several animals. Long before the rise of Greek civilization, multispecies monsters were found in Middle Eastern mythology, such as the Sphinx, whose image appeared first as a sculpture in Turkey and then as the largest statue in the world in Giza, Egypt, thousands of years before the time of Homer. Another example is the Chimera—part snake, part lion, and part goat—which first appeared in Hittite lore and formed the basis for all Greek monsters of this type. They may have been so popular because they were easy for storytellers to think up, similar to the present-day jokes along the lines of "Whaddaya get when you cross a giant chicken with an armadillo wearing Donald Trump's hair?"

Other kinds of mythical monsters are the spirits of natural phenomena, which either take on their own per-sonalities (the way some people today talk about Hurricane Katrina) or become guardians of wild places like the nymphs of forests, streams, and mountains. Related to these are monsters that bring particular landmarks (usually dangerous ones) to life, like Scylla and Charybdis, who imperil sailors from their rock formations in the Mediterranean Sea. Still others are giants, throwbacks to an earlier time when they ruled the earth, often with little in the way of brains but plenty of brawn.

Among the most intriguing types of monsters in Greek mythology were the automatons, creatures manufactured out of bronze—usually by the metalworking god Hephaestus—and then brought to life. In the Bronze Age, when shaping objects from metal was the height of human technology, automatons tended to represent the power and peril of manmade beings run amok. This has often been a preoccupation throughout Western literature, as we can in such science fiction classics as Mary Shelley's *Frankenstein,* H. G. Wells's *The Island of Doctor Moreau,* or Isaac Asimov's *I, Robot.*

The rogues' gallery of Greek and Roman monsters even includes a few human serial killers such as Procrustes, whose hospitality habits made him as unsavory as Hannibal Lecter. On the other hand, some of the creatures of Greek monster lore—like the Gray Sisters, who possess fewer eyes between them than a family of Cyclopes—come across as less fearsome than just plain goofy.

The brief entries on the following pages will give you some idea of the full range of unnatural creatures waiting for you to discover in Greek and Roman mythology. Have fun!

✳ ✳ ✳ ✳

ANEMI THUELLAI

Anemi Thuellai, the spirits of violent storms, could appear either as ghostly young men with pale wings and electric eyes or phantom horses charged with electricity. Zeus placed these spirits in the hands of Aiolos the wind god to let them loose upon the world as needed. They could knock a hero off his feet or shoot lightning bolts at him. If the hero caught them while still in their terrestrial form, he could stab them with his celestial weapon, and they'd disintegrate like any monster. Once they'd transformed into wind and lightning, they could only be defeated by plowing through them with another wind element, as Jason does in *The Lost Hero*.

✻ ✻ ✻ ✻

ANTAEUS

A son of Poseidon and Gaea, Antaeus would force visitors passing through his land to wrestle with him. As long as he could stay in contact with the ground, he was invincible. He took the skulls of all those he defeated to make the roof to a temple he built in honor of his father. Heracles weakened him by

Heracles lifting Antaeus off the ground.

lifting him off the ground, then crushed his ribs and killed him. In *The Battle of the Labyrinth*, Percy Jackson and his companions are waylaid in his territory, which has become part of the Labyrinth, a sprawling underground world full of mythic surprises. Percy doesn't wrestle Antaeus to death as Heracles had, but does defeat him by separating him from the ground.

❈ ❈ ❈ ❈

AGRIUS & OREIUS

These twin brothers, half-human and half-bear, stood fully eight feet tall. They were covered in fur and had paws for feet, claws for fingernails, and bearlike snouts and fangs. They also liked to eat humans. Their mother, Polyphonte, had worshipped Aphrodite but then switched her allegiance to Artemis, taking a vow of chastity. In revenge, Aphrodite caused a bear to rape her, and the offspring were Agrius and Oreius. Percy Jackson and friends confront the bear twins twice in *The Sea of Monsters* and discover that, notwithstanding their size and ferocity, their weakness lies in the fact that they are as stupid as boxes of rocks.

❈ ❈ ❈ ❈

BOREAS

Boreas, the Greek god of the North Wind and winter, would sweep down from the mountains and chill the air with his icy breath. He had purple wings, and his hair and beard were spiked with ice; he was sometimes depicted as a horse. His daughter Khione was the goddess of snow. As Jason, Piper, and Leo find out *The Lost Hero*, Boreas can be either an ally or an enemy. He has been known to be helpful to demigods in the past. Today his name lives on the spectacular colored lights that appear in the northern skies during winter, the aurora borealis.

❋ ❋ ❋ ❋

BRIAREUS

Briareus was one of the three giant storm gods known as the Hecatoncheires, meaning "hundred-handed." Each of them also had fifty heads. They were brothers of the first three Cyclopes, and their father, Uranus, kept them imprisoned in the pit of Tartarus until Zeus set them free to help him wage his war against the Titan gods. After the war, Zeus rewarded them with palaces in the depths of the Aegean Sea. Percy, Grover, Annabeth, and Tyson encounter Briareus when, in the *The Battle of the Labyrinth*, they found him imprisoned in Alcatraz. They free him, and he joins their side.

✖ ✖ ✖ ✖

CARCINUS

Carcinus was a giant crab whose only appearance in ancient Greek myth was when it attacked Heracles, who was battling the Lernaean Hydra. His arms busy with swordplay, Heracles nevertheless managed to crush the monster beneath his feet. Hera honored the crab by placing it among the stars as a constellation, where it is known as Cancer. Like many slain monsters, Carcinus eventually came back to life, and Percy Jackson has his own run-in with it in *The Last Olympian*. Although he lacks Heracles's weight and strength, Percy manages to defeat the monster crab in his own way.

❋ ❋ ❋ ❋

COLCHIS BULLS

This matched pair of fire-breathing bulls was made of bronze by the fire god Hephaestus as a gift for the king of Colchis. During his quest for the Golden Fleece, the hero Jason was ordered by the king to yoke the bulls like oxen and plow the king's field before he would consent to hand over the fleece. The king's daughter, Medea, offered to help Jason if he agreed to marry her. When he said yes, she gave him a salve that made him impervious to fire and iron for a day. Thus protected, he was able to complete the task and retrieve the Golden Fleece. The marriage didn't last, though. Percy Jackson meets the robot bulls in *Sea of Monsters*.

❋ ❋ ❋ ❋

DRACAENA SCYTHIA

The Dragon Lady of Scythia appeared to be a normal woman from the waist up but had the snakelike body of a drakon from the waist down. She is said to have forced the hero Heracles to father three sons with her by stealing his horses when he passed through her lands and only returning them if he agreed to have intimate relations with her.

In the Roman version, she had two serpent tails, one in place of each leg, making Hercules's dalliance with her only slightly less gross. Percy Jackson encounters (but of course does not get physical with) a similar she-serpent in *The Sea of Monsters*.

※ ※ ※ ※

EMPUSA

This flame-haired, shapeshifting demigoddess had one leg made of brass, while the other was that of a donkey. She and her sisters could disguise themselves as beautiful women to seduce men in their sleep before sucking their blood. Empusa was said to be a creation of Hecate, the goddess of witchcraft, magic, and ghosts, who sent her out in the world to frighten travelers. Percy Jackson first runs into her and her sisters dressed as cheerleaders in *The Battle of the Labyrinth*, and they reappear throughout the series. They live on in modern Greek folklore as creatures similar to vampires.

※ ※ ※ ※

ENCELADUS

One of the giant sons of Gaea and Tartarus, Enceladus was a hundred-armed giant who took part in the original giant war against the gods of Olympus. He was bronzed from the waist up and covered in green scales from the waist down. Instead of hands and feet he had the claws of a drakon, and he could breathe fire. Since his name translates as "sound the charge," his appearance is a signal that a war is about to begin. Enceladus confronts Jason, Piper, and Leo in *The Lost Hero* and promises he will be back. One of the moons of the planet Saturn is named after him.

ERINYES

These ugly winged women with mouths full of yellow fangs, claws for fingers, and hair, arms, and waists entwined with poisonous snakes were servants of Hades in the Underworld, where they oversaw the torture of criminals. Even in the earthly realm, invoking their names could bring a curse of vengeance for certain serious crimes—crimes against the natural order, homicide, mistreatment of parents, crimes against the gods, and perjury. Otherwise they were generally friendly to the Olympian gods. Known by the Romans as the Furies, one or more of them puts in appearances in both *The Lightning Thief* and *The Last Olympian*.

ERYMANTHIAN BOAR

Heracles was assigned to capture this gigantic wild boar, which was destroying farmlands in the ancient Greek kingdom of Arkadia, and bring it back alive to King Eurystheus. He succeeded in doing so by chasing the boar into a deep snowbank. When he brought it to court, it is said that the king was so terrified by the sight of the creature that he leaped into a huge storage jug for safety. Later, several Roman legions used the boar as their emblem, signifying courage and ferocity in battle. Percy Jackson and company meet the boar, an encounter that turns out to be a blessing, in *The Titan's Curse*.

Heracles captures the wild Erymanthian boar.

GEGENEES

This band of six-armed giants, whose name means "earthborn" because their mother was Gaea, battled Jason and the Argonauts during their voyages. They were not very big as giants go, standing about seven feet tall, but they did have lots of arms—two apiece growing from their shoulders and four more from their torsos. They were strong but none too bright, so they were vulnerable to trickery. In *The Lost Hero*, Jason, the ancient hero's modern namesake, and his companions Piper and Leo faces off against the Gegenees, who are portrayed as somewhat childlike.

❋ ❋ ❋ ❋

GERYON

Geryon, a three-bodied giant, had the usual two arms, two legs, and one head on three torsos attached side by side. His left arm attached at the shoulder to the left torso and the right the same on the other side, with the head riding on the middle atop his neck. Why? Because if a hero stabbed him in one of his hearts, the other two bodies could keep on fighting until the third one had healed. One of the labors assigned to Heracles was to slay Geryon and take his cattle herd. Percy Jackson meets the giant in *The Battle of the Labyrinth*, where Geryon appears as a trader of monsters.

❋ ❋ ❋ ❋

GRAY SISTERS

Called Graeae by the Greeks, these three old-woman sea demons were named for their gray color. In Roman versions, there were only two of them, but as in many mythic traditions, three witches are better than two. The living personification of the white foam of the sea, they shared a single tooth and eye between the three of them—a handicap with endless comic possibilities. The most dangerous thing about them was their formidable-sounding names: Deino ("the dread"), Enyo ("the warlike"), and Persis ("the destroyer"). In *The Sea of Monsters,* they appear as cab drivers and reveal a vital bit of information to Percy Jackson.

HELLHOUNDS

"Hellhounds" is actually a generic term used to describe many canine creatures associated with evil deeds. In his Percy Jackson & the Olympians series, author Rick Riordan has created a monster that incorporates various elements of different Hellhounds from folklore, which are described as being large, black-furred, and generally vicious. Percy Jackson meets one in *The Lightning Thief* and another much larger one in *The Battle of the Labyrinth*. Fortunately, the latter—a tank-sized beast who goes by the name of Mrs. O'Leary—is literally a teacher's pet who turns out to be friendly and becomes Percy's devoted companion.

HIPPOCAMPI

Hippocampi, magical creatures of the sea, were hybrids of horses and fish. Some were described as having the head and forelegs of a horse, while others were depicted more like fish with horses' heads, often covered in green scales with fish-fin manes and fins instead of legs. A team of four pulled Poseidon's chariot. The ancients believed them to be the adult form of the creature we now know as the sea horse, whose scientific genus is also named hippocampus. As the son of Poseidon, Percy Jackson naturally has a good relationship with Hippocampi and in *The Sea of Monsters* he frequently calls upon them for rides in the ocean.

HYPERBOREAN GIANTS

The full name of these giants was Boreades Hyperboreioi, reflecting their heritage as the sons of Boreas, the god of the north wind, and Khione, who was not his daughter, the goddess of snow, but a snow nymph of the same name whom the god loved. They were huge, around 30 feet tall, but not particularly belligerent. In addition to their strength and immense size, they also had the ability to turn areas to ice using their breath. Percy Jackson has a brief run-in with one of the giants in *The Last Olympian,* and in the same book another one serves as a herald to the Titan Prometheus in a parley.

❈ ❈ ❈ ❈

KAMPÊ

This particularly nasty monster had the body of a woman from the waist up, with serpents covering her head instead of hair. From the waist down she had the body of a scaly drakon with a thousand vipers for feet, and sprouting from her waist were the heads of 50 fearsome beasts, all alive and each perfectly capable of taking a bite out of an adversary. Large, batlike leathery wings sprouted from her shoulders, and she was further armed with a scorpion's stinger tail.

In the Roman version, her eyes shot sparks, and the viper feet spat poison. When Percy Jackson and crew first meet up with Kampê in *The Battle of the Labyrinth,* they wisely avoid her, though the second time they aren't so lucky.

LADON

Also known as the Hesperius Drakon because he was tasked to guard the golden apples in the Garden of Hesperides, Ladon had a hundred heads, and a bite from any of them was poisonous. As one of his 12 labors, Heracles was sent to steal the golden apples and in the process slew Ladon. When Jason and the Argonauts passed the apple tree 15 years later, the dragon's corpse was still twitching. As the apples had been Hera's wedding present from Zeus, she honored their protector after his death by placing him among the stars as the constellation Draco. Percy Jackson gives Ladon a wide berth in *The Titan's Curse.*

LUPA & LYCAON

Lupa, the Latin word for she-wolf, refers to the mother wolf who reared Romulus and Remus, the legendary founders of Rome. Lycaon represents the evil characteristics humans

have attributed to wolves: That they're evil, man-eating shapeshifters. His name comes from the word "lycan-thropes," meaning werewolves. Lupa was a pure wolf, while Lycaon, the King of the Wolves, could transform from a man to a wolf at will. These two are strictly Roman creatures that did not appear in Greek mythology. In *The Lost Hero*, Lupa appears to Jason in a dream to help guide him in figuring out his history and discovering his path. Later, Jason, Piper, and Leo have a near-fatal showdown with Lycaon.

❊ ❊ ❊ ❊

NEREUS

Also known as the Old Man of the Sea, Nereus was the god of the fish caught at sea. He was said to be a master shapeshifter, which made it very difficult to find him. As he was also a prophet, people would often seek him out to learn what he knew, but he wouldn't surrender his knowledge willingly. Heracles was forced to wrestle Nereus when he wanted directions to the land of the Hesperides. Sometimes Nereus is pictured as having a fish tail instead of legs and clothed in scales. In *The Titan's Curse*, Percy Jackson finds it challenging to get a straight answer out of him.

❇ ❇ ❇ ❇

NYMPHS

Nymphai, or nymphs in English, were divine nature spirits, though not gods. They presided over everything from freshwater springs to clouds, cooling breezes, forests, caverns, mountains, meadows, beaches, and the sea. Their primary concern was with the welfare of those elements and they used natural "weapons" that ranged from windstorms to giant waves and whirlpools against anyone who might hurt what was under their protection. Most often they were associated with gods who reigned over nature, such as Hermes, Dionysus, Artemis, Poseidon, Demeter, and Pan. Nymphs fight to save the environment in *The Lightning Thief, The Battle of the Labyrinth,* and *The Lost Hero.*

❇ ❇ ❇ ❇

OPHIOTAUROS

With the foreparts of a black bull and the tail of a snake, Ophiotauros ("serpent bull") must have made an odd sight swimming through the seas. Odder yet, while it was a harmless creature in itself, it posed the greatest threat to the survival of the Olympian gods in their war against the Titans, for it was foretold that whoever sacrificed this creature would be destined to defeat the gods. Thus, the threat from Ophiotauros lay not in what it could do but in the temptation that it offered. Percy Jackson first meets the Ophiotauros in *The Titan's Curse*, but it's his friend Thalia who faces the temptation to sacrifice it.

❇ ❇ ❇ ❇

PROCRUSTES

Procrustes was a human with a monstrous habit. He would waylay travelers on the road to Athens and offer them his bed of iron to sleep in for the night. But while they were asleep, he would "adjust" them to fit in the bed properly. He would stretch those who were too short until they were the right length and, using his sword, shorten those who had the misfortune of being too tall for his bed, removing whatever length of leg was required for them to fit snugly. He was eventually slain by the hero Theseus, but though

he was mortal, his demise was apparently not permanent;
Percy Jackson encounters Procrustes on his first quest in
The Lightning Thief.

✖ ✖ ✖ ✖

SPHINX

A giant creature with the head of a woman, the body of a
lion, the wings of an eagle, and a serpent-headed tail, this
ancient creature is more often associated with Egypt, but

it has appeared in many
mythologies since the
first sphinx sculpture was
erected in Turkey around
9500 B.C. In Greek my-
thology it waylaid travelers, refusing to let them
pass unless they could
answer the riddle, "What
is it that has one voice and
is four-footed, two-footed,
and three-footed?" Those
who failed to answer cor-

rectly had to find an alternate route or be eaten alive. In *The
Battle of the Labyrinth,* Annabeth discovers that the riddle

has been changed over the years. (A similar thing happens in J. K. Rowling's *Harry Potter and the Goblet of Fire.*)

❋❋❋❋

STYMPHALIAN BIRDS

Beware the flock of man-eating pigeons named for the lake they haunted, Lake Stymphalis. Though relatively small creatures, they would swarm when attacking and, like the deadly piranha fish of the Amazon, could quickly strip the flesh from their victim. It was the hero Heracles who destroyed the original flock as the sixth of his 12 labors. He used a large rattle to scare them out of their roosts among the trees around the lake, and then shot them one by one with an arrow or a slingshot. Percy Jackson uses much the same tactic when the birds attack him during a chariot race at Camp Half-Blood in *The Sea of Monsters.*

❋❋❋❋

TALOS

Manufactured by the fire god Hephaestus, Talos was a huge, bronze, man-shaped automaton—in other words, an ancient robot—that Zeus gave to Europa, one of his human lovers, as a personal protector while she lived on the island of Crete. The giant patrolled the island and drove enemies away with volleys of rocks. He also had the power to make himself burn red-hot and kill strangers by embracing them. Talos's only vulnerability was the same as that of the hero Achilles. In *The Titan's Curse*, Percy Jackson and other demigods defeat Talos during their quest to rescue Annabeth, but the fight costs one of their company her life.

❋ ❋ ❋ ❋

TYPHON

This monstrous, immortal storm-giant was said to have been so huge his head brushed the stars. Man-shaped to his thighs, Typhon had two coiled vipers in place of his legs; 50 serpent heads on each hand instead of fingers; giant wings; dirty, matted hair and beard; pointed ears; and eyes that flashed fire. He hurled red-hot rocks at the sky and storms of fire boiled from his mouth. In the original giant wars, he actually captured and imprisoned Zeus, who was rescued by his sons. If you doubt that Typhon is the most dangerous monster in this chapter, read about how he blows up Mount St. Helens in *The Battle of the Labyrinth*. He also appears in *The Lost Hero*.

CHAPTER SIX

The New Series Begins

WHAT IF SOMEONE claimed they could predict what the future held in store for you? Would you let them tell you? And if they told you, would you then accept everything they said as guaranteed and do nothing to try to change your destiny?

Some people believe that even before you're born, the path of your life has been decided, and every choice you make has been preordained by some higher power. No matter what you do or how hard you try to change it, it won't matter—you'll live your life according to this destiny. Others believe that we each have the potential to shape our own lives, and the choices we make shape our fate. Regardless of philosophy, though, people throughout history have tried to learn how their lives will turn out. Today people consult psychics, read horoscopes or tarot cards, cast the *I Ching*, or use any number of other methods—including genetic testing—to try to glean some small glimpse of what's to come.

Predicting the Future for Fun and Profit

In one form or another, prophecy and prediction have been practiced all over the world for many thousands of years. In classical Greece and Rome, people set great store by prophecies and omens. No one, not even an emperor or the general of an army, would dream of making a decision without first consulting with a soothsayer, seer, or oracle. Only after such a consultation would people decide if someone was the right person for them to marry, if it was a good time to make a business deal, or if the signs were auspicious to declare war on another nation. In both Greece and Rome, Apollo was the god of oracles, and the most important of the seven major oracles was located at Delphi, in the mountains of central Greece west of Athens. People would make pilgrimages to Delphi to find out what the future held for them or how they could win the favor of the gods, whereupon they would be instructed to sacrifice livestock as offerings to the gods or perform some difficult task to prove themselves.

The word "oracle" meant both the place and the chief priest or priestess through whose lips the prophetic words were spoken. Often, the meanings of the prophecies weren't very clear. Like riddles, they might only make sense after they had come true. Yet people who believed in predestination would value any hint that might help them see where their lives were going.

In Rick Riordan's world of Percy Jackson & the Olympians and Heroes of Olympus, those who live in both everyday and mythic worlds set great store in the old ways. Burnt offerings to the gods are offered with every meal, and oaths are sworn in the name of the appropriate god or goddess. Respect for omens and prophecies holds sway over the books' characters, whether mortal, immortal, magical, or monstrous. Even the gods allow these predictions to shape their worlds.

There are two kinds of prophecies: big, earth-shaking ones that can span decades or even centuries, and smaller ones that apply to specific events or circumstances. In Percy Jackson & the Olympians, one Great Prophecy has been guiding the actions of the gods for decades:

> *A half-blood of the eldest gods*
> *Shall reach sixteen against all odds,*
> *And see the world in endless sleep,*

The hero's soul, cursed blade shall reap.
A single choice shall and his days.
Olympus to preserve or raze.
—*The Last Olympian*, pp 55–56

While neither Percy nor the reader hears it in its entirety until the final book of the series *(The Last Olympian),* we understand enough of it to know that a half-mortal child of the "eldest gods" (Zeus, Poseidon, or Hades—referred to as the "Big Three" in the series), will do something at age 16 to decide the fate of Olympus and all the gods. For this reason the three gods swore a pact not to have any more demigod children—but Greek gods aren't always good at keeping their oaths. Thus the prophecy becomes the driving force behind the series.

The odd thing about prophecies is how easy it is for anybody, including the gods, to either misinterpret them or read what they want into them. Nearly all the action in the Percy Jackson & the Olympians series is motivated by somebody's interpretation of this one prophecy. Everything the young demigods do and each quest they undertake happens because of it. It's easy to see why nobody is too thrilled that the Great Prophecy was made. Then, as the original prophecy plays out at the end of *The Last Olympian,* a newly appointed Oracle of Delphi delivers another one, consisting of just four lines that sound like not-very-good poetry:

Seven half-bloods shall answer the call.
To storm or fire, the world must fall.
An oath to keep with a final breath,
And foes to bear arms to the Doors of Death.
  —*The Last Olympian*, p. 368

People are a little disconcerted, and the next series of novels is off and running.

When you consider how much of the plot of the first series revolves around a single prediction, it stands to reason that the new Great Prophecy, along with any additional information the oracle may able to channel, will go a long way toward pointing the new heroes (Piper, Leo, and Jason) in the right direction. Prophecies may or may not be self-fulfilling, but in Rick Riordan's world, it's a good bet that they'll always come true—though not necessarily in the manner anybody expected.

THE FUTURE OF THE HEROES OF OLYMPUS

In the tradition of oracles of old, the Internet abounds with fans' speculations about what will happen next in the Heroes of Olympus series. Rick Riordan and his publishers have already released two volumes of a planned trilogy called the Kane Chronicles, set in a fictional modern-day universe based on Egyptian mythology, with the final volume, so-far untitled, scheduled for publication in May 2012; but Percy Jackson and his pals are not mentioned in it. Many readers hope that Rick Riordan will tackle the world of Norse myth next, though there's no evidence that this will happen, merely wishful thinking. Yet Riordan and his publishers have remained exceptionally secretive about all the forthcoming Heroes of Olympus books, making it hard to guess what we may find in even the second novel, *The Son of Neptune.*

What we can say for sure about the Heroes of Olympus series is that it introduces three new lead characters, shifting viewpoints between them and telling their story in the third person (unlike the earlier Percy Jackson series). They fit the mold of most of the 20th century's adolescent hero teams: *Peter Pan's* Wendy, John, and Michael Darling; *Narnia's* Peter, Susan, Edmund, and Lucy Pevensie; J. K. Rowling's Harry Potter, Hermione Granger, and Ron Weasley; and of course Percy Jackson, Annabeth Chase, and Grover Underwood of the earlier Percy Jackson & the Olympians series.

The new heroes' leader is Jason Grace, who is named after the Greek hero Jason, just as Percy Jackson was named after Perseus. He possesses sharply honed fighting skills from his past training in the Roman counterpart to Camp Half-Blood, though amnesia prevents him from remembering the training or the camp itself. Piper McLean is a departure from Riordan's previous gutsy female heroes, such as Annabeth and Clarissa. Her mother raised her to be a Barbie doll, so to speak. But as an heir of Aphrodite, she has one irresistable superpower: Her words can charm anyone into anything. Leo Valdez comes across as a sort of sidekick character who handles many of the day-to-day chores—cooking meals, repairing equipment, arranging transportation—that his fellow questers are too preoccupied with heroic concerns to think about. His skills with fire and metalworking, along with his quick wit, make him the glue that holds the new team together.

It's no secret that Percy Jackson is still around somewhere. Though he's barely mentioned in the first book of the new series, *The Lost Hero,* he *is* the "lost hero" of the title. He's also the "son of Neptune" in the forthcoming *The Son of Neptune.* The front cover art for that book, which was released by the publisher before the author had completed writing the novel, depicts a soaked, bedraggled Percy scrambling onto an ice floe. In the background is a towering glacier with toppling temples on top, which tells us he's probably no longer in upstate New York. He is clutching a staff with a gold eagle on top, a good indication that he's with the Romans now. The title, too, suggests a Roman theme with its reference to Percy's father as Neptune rather than the Greek version, Poseidon.

At the same time the book cover was unveiled, Rick Riordan released a preview—the first chapter of *The Son of Neptune*—which describes a battle between a dazed and confused Percy and Medusa's immortal Gorgon sisters, Euryale and Stheno, in the streets of the San Francisco Bay Area. Both sisters appear exclusively in Greek myth, not Roman, and have Greek names. But the chapter does not reveal any further hints about where the plot of the new book may lead, and some fans have even suggested that it may be some sort of dream sequence, put out by the publisher's marketing department as a red herring to keep readers guessing.

The advance teasers for *The Son of Neptune* may offer less basis for intelligent guesswork than for frustration. The four-line prophecy in *The Lost Hero* suggests, among other things, that a seventh young demigod hero, as yet

The first chapter of The Son of Neptune *describes a battle between Percy and the Gorgons in San Francisco.*

unidentified, will join the three (Jason, Piper, and Leo) we've met so far. Otherwise, no clues at all are offered to the storyline of the later novels in the series—not even their working titles—except that there will be three more volumes after *The Son of Neptune*.

If you want to speculate on what tales may come in the future books of the series, one place to start might be the Roman writings of antiquity. Some fans speculate that, just as the Percy Jackson & the Olympians series drew heavily on mythical characters from Homer's *The Iliad* and *The Odyssey*, the new series might use Virgil's *Aeneid* as a central source. This epic poem, written in Latin during the reign of Augustus Caesar, was designed to emphasize the link between Roman mythology and the earlier, still-respected Greek culture, as well as to prove that the founding fathers of Rome

The Greek poet Homer.

were of Trojan descent. It covers a lot of the same territory as Homer's Greek epics, and the writing style of *The Aeneid* is at least as dense and cryptic as that of *The Iliad*, such that even the most sadistic of high school teachers rarely require their students to read much of it. It begins:

> *Arms, and the man I sing, who, forc'd by fate, and*
> *haughty Juno's unrelenting hate, expell'd and*
> *exil'd, left the Trojan shore. Long labors, both by sea*

*and land, he bore, and in the doubtful war, before
he won the Latian realm, and built the destin'd
town; his banish'd gods restor'd to rites divine, and
settled sure succession in his line, from whence the
race of Alban fathers come, and the long glories of
majestic Rome.*

Oh, well, it may be hard to figure out exactly what
Virgil was saying, but at least it rhymes and has the kind of
rhythm that would fit a modern rock song.

Another Romanization of Greek mythology, *Metamorphosis*, written by the poet Ovid in the year A.D. 8,
is often called a mock-epic, in that it does not so much
deal with battles and heroes as satirize the concept of love,
jumping from myth to myth without much transition. It,
too, rhymes:

*Of bodies chang'd to various forms, I sing: Ye Gods,
from whom these miracles did spring, inspire my
numbers with coelestial heat;*

*Till I my long laborious work compleat: and add
perpetual tenour to my rhimes, deduc'd from Nature's birth, to Caesar's times. Before the seas, and
this terrestrial ball, and Heav'n's high canopy,
that covers all, one was the face of Nature; if a face:
rather a rude and indigested mass: a lifeless lump,
unfashion'd, and unfram'd, of jarring seeds; and
justly Chaos nam'd.*

"Huh?" you may well say. If you choose to go this route in your quest for hints about Rick Riordan's heroes' future exploits, be careful to get a copy of Ovid's *Metamorphosis*, not German author Franz Kafka's novella of the same name, or you'll be in for a completely different weird reading experience about a traveling salesman who turns into a giant cockroach, which sounds like it could be some kind of Greek monster—but it's not.

You may find more accessible hints about the mythological content of Riordan's novels in a children's book (ages 9–12) called *The Golden Fleece and the Heroes Who Lived Before Achilles*, written by Irish-American poet Padraic Colum and originally published in 1921. This book was rereleased in 2010 with a new introduction by Rick Riordan himself, though it has a different publisher from the Percy Jackson books. It deals with the legend of Jason and the Argonauts, and since this is the same hero who inspired the character of Jason Grace in the Heroes of Olympus series, it makes sense that at least some of the events in future novels of the series will echo the myths that Colum's book retells.

You Never Know What's Going to Happen—Even When It Already Did

How the adventures of the Heroes of Olympus will come about and what's going to happen to the individual characters remains up in the air. We know that Rick Riordan has been scrupulous in his re-creations of those elements of the classical world he included in both Percy Jackson & the Olympians and The Heroes of Olympus. Whether retelling the stories and adventures of ancient heroes with Percy, Annabeth, Jason, Piper, Leo and the rest filling in for the great Greek heroes of old, describing and representing the gods and goddesses as they interact with each other and the rest of the world, or depicting the ancient Greek and Roman cultures, he has been unfailing in his attention to detail. Everything, from how to slay monsters to the types of weapons and armor worn in ancient Greece and Rome, is either historically correct or at least faithful to events described in the original myths.

This is why we've done our best to arm you with knowledge about Greco-Roman mythology. The more you know about it, the better you can predict what will happen. Knowing details about our heroes' immortal parents ensures a deeper understanding of who they are and what they're capable of doing, since each hero has inherited something of his or her immortal parent's power, and there's a good chance they share some of their personality quirks as well. At the very least, this type of information should offer insights into how a hero will react under a variety of conditions. If a son of Zeus/Jupiter is challenged, will he back down and give way, or will he stand up to whatever is facing him, regardless of the odds?

Of course, there are still a host of monsters out there that our heroes haven't run into yet. There are indications in *The Lost Hero* that they'll be spending quite a bit of their time traveling by sea, so chances are they'll meet up with sea creatures or ones who live on islands. Chances are they'll also be seeing familiar faces along the way, perhaps some that Percy has encountered before but Jason and his crew have not.

Other material that Rick Riordan could draw on as inspiration for adventures might include Greek theatre. The Greeks invented the play as a storytelling form, and in some cases playwrights' works contain the only surviving accounts of events or offer versions that are far more detailed than those found anywhere else.

No matter what the setting, whether the heroes are fighting for their lives or merely hanging out at Camp Half-Blood, Rick Riordan has done an amazing job of creating a world where the gods, goddesses, and assorted other strange and bizarre beings of Greece and Rome are not only alive but as easy to believe in as any mortal being. As

The Greeks used plays as a means of storytelling, and their works may offer insight into future Heroes of Olympus books.

a reader, after a while you start to take the fantastic for granted, as if you, too, had spent a lot of time hanging out with a Centaur and had a Cyclops for a half-brother. Like Percy Jackson, we might have started out not knowing very much about this alternate reality, but with each passing adventure, we learn more and more about it. Like pieces in a jigsaw puzzle, each new bit of information slots into the overall picture of events controlling the lives of the characters and the world in which they live.

By holding up each puzzle piece up to the light and examining it closely, it becomes possible to see that pattern behind how they fit together. While following the pattern might not provide us with specific answers about how the Heroes of Olympus series will play out, it can give us clues as to the direction the books be taking. At the same time, we hope this information will enhance the experience of being in the mythic world of magic, gods, and monsters Rick Riordan has created, and most of all, we hope this readers' companion adds to your enjoyment of the books.

ARTWORK CREDITS

Index of Gods and Monsters

Acknowledgments

Natalie Buczynsky: Thanks to Brent Cole, a more experienced fellow author, for all of his help in guiding me through the legalities of publishing and for his special "magic sauce." I thank my mom for being encouraging and uplifting, and my dad for helping me navigate the world of professionals. I'd also like to thank Richard Marcus and Jonathan Shelnutt for being wonderful, supportive coauthors. Thanks to Keith Riegert, for taking a chance on two unknown high school writers. A huge thanks goes out to the staff at percyquest.com and especially to Julia and Kyle. Last but certainly not least, a huge thanks goes to the rest of my encouraging family and friends, especially Anna Sophia, for coaching me through my initial writer's block. These people and so many more helped make this book a reality.

Jonathan Shelnutt: Thank you to Natalie Buczynsky, who has done far more than her share in making this book possible. Keith Riegert and Richard Marcus have been great companions on this journey. Keith went out on a limb for me, and Richard has been the voice of experience. Thanks to my hardworking parents and four wonderful sisters, who have supported me every step of the way. I'd like to acknowledge every writing teacher I've ever had, but two in particular: my mother, who patiently taught me to coax coherent speech out of the cacophony of my brain; and Mrs. Weinrich, who has provided a structure into which I can pour the hurricane of words in my imagination. And last, but not least, I'd like to acknowledge you, the reader. Without your dedication, none of this would be possible. In its own way, this book is a little miracle of humanity.

Richard Marcus: Thank you to authors and friends Ashok Banker and Robert Scott, who have been unstinting in their support and encouragement. To Eric Olsen and Lisa McKay, former publisher and managing editor of Blogcritics.org, respectively, who created a space and atmosphere that encouraged creativity. To Robert Lecker, my agent, who took me on for a project that has yet to get off the ground, but he stuck around, for which I'm continually grateful. Thank you to Keith Riegert, Richard Harris, and everyone else at Ulysses Press. To my mother, Susan Marcus, and my brother, David Chalmers, who have seen the worst of me and still let me hang around. To my wife Eriana Marcus, who still doesn't seem to be sick of me after fifteen years, for which I'm always grateful. Finally, to Richard Riordan. Thank you for your imagination and talent—without them there would have been nothing for us to write about.

About the Authors

NATALIE BUCZYNSKY, a high school student from Georgia, is the web mistress and head writer for percyquest.com. She has written many editorials including, "The Lightning Thief vs. the Red Pyramid," "Greek and Egyptian Mythology," and "Predictions for the Next Camp Half-Blood Series." She has also written four short stories and runs an advice column based from percyquest.com. She's enjoyed studying Ancient Greek and Latin and has translated John and First John from their original Biblical text. Natalie hopes to write for a magazine such as *Teen Girl*, *American Girl*, or *Seventeen* one day. When she's not writing, she loves hanging out with her friends at coffee shops and bookstores.

JONATHAN SHELNUTT, a high school student living in Athens, Georgia, has loved Greek mythology for as long as he can remember. He has four spectacular sisters, two loving parents, and a diverse group of close friends. An experienced actor, archer, and writer, Jonathan's favorite Greek god is Apollo, but he respects Athena the most. Jonathan has been a Percy Jackson fan ever since his friend gave him the first four books for his twelfth birthday, and has memorized more Percy Jackson trivia than he'd like to admit. He owes the honor of writing this guide to his classmate Natalie Buczynsky, a fellow addict of Greek myths. Jonathan is an expert at deciphering Greek myths and the Percy Jackson series in particular.

RICHARD MARCUS is the author of *What Will Happen in Eragon IV?* (Ulysses Press), editor of the online southeast Asian arts and culture site *Epic India Magazine*, and has been a contributor to the online pop culture magazine Blogcritics.org since 2006. He has been published in international media, including the German edition of *Rolling Stone* magazine. Richard runs his own blog, *Leap In The Dark*. A prolific writer of both fiction and nonfiction, he lives in Eastern Ontario, Canada, with his wife, poet/artist/musician Eriana Marcus, and their three cats.

The Twelve Olympians

GREEK	ROMAN
Aphrodite	Venus
Apollo	Apollo
Ares	Mars
Artemis	Diana
Athena	Minerva
Demeter	Ceres
Dionysus	Bacchus
Hephaestus	Vulcan
Hera	Juno
Hermes	Mercury
Poseidon	Neptune
Zeus	Jupiter